The Life and Times of Wolfram of Eschenbach

by

J. Wesley Thomas

FIRST EDITION

Library of Congress Catalog Card No: 06-90238
ISBN: 1-56002-668-5

UNIVERSITY EDITIONS, Inc.
59 Oak Lane, Spring Valley
Huntington, West Virginia 25704

Cover by Anna Finkel

Dedication

To Lina

her wolfran von Eschilbach. ·xlvij·

Prologue

"I am most grateful that you were so kind as to grant me an interview," I told the grey ghost who was sitting on a weathered gravestone before me. "I had heard that you sometimes were seen here on bright summer nights, but I hardly dared hope that you would heed my invocation."

"I was intrigued that a man of the twentieth century should address me in my own medieval speech," was the reply. "Actually, you handle it rather well; the intonation is not quite right, but your grammar is perfect. I hope you are not disappointed in me. Now and then, in the later years of my life, an enthusiastic devotee of Parzival, Gawain, and Willehalm would arrive to visit the grave of the famous poet who put their stories into German verse. But when the pilgrim found in place of a shrine an ancient rustic who not only had the poor taste to outlive his time but also belied conventional concepts of a romancer, he left promptly, resentful at being so deceived. Still, I suppose a ghost of any kind is more noteworthy than an old village squire. Well, here I am. What is it that you wish to know?"

"Everything, Sir Wolfram, everything!" I said. "Many scholars maintain that you were the greatest epic poet between Vergil and Dante, but, whereas the lives of the Roman and the Florentine are known in detail, no historical document so much as mentions the pride of Eschenbach. We scholars have pieced together a scanty biography from the names of people and places in your works, but even that little is controversial. I would learn all about your life and also hear what you have to say about your times. As a knight, a poet, a fief holder, and a guest at many courts, you certainly can throw much light on the most important period of the Middle Ages."

"To be sure, I lived in extraordinary times," he answered. "I observed—usually, but not always, from afar—the Welf-Hohenstaufen struggle to head the Holy Roman Empire, the two German Crusades in the Holy Land, the efforts of the Hohenstaufens to retain control of Italy, and other such matters as concerned a king and four emperors. Moreover I knew the songs, romances, and tales of the period and heard many episodes as fact that later became popular folklore. If you are a student of what you call the Middle Ages, you may be acquainted with different versions of them, but you can believe my accounts, for I was there, and my memory of all that transpired during my life is excellent, although it is quite hazy about subsequent events. I may even sing for you some of the songs that were popular then. Now pray do not interrupt me, for this might cause me to lose my train of thought."

Then the ghost began the following account and talked on throughout the moon-lit night, while I struggled with paper and pencil to record it all. It was just starting to get light when he halted expectantly, like an actor on a stage. When I applauded enthusiastically, he stood up, bowed, and vanished.

Eschenbach and Wertheim

I, Sir Wolfram, was born in 1170 above the Franconian village of Eschenbach, where my father, Sir Eberhard, was lord of the modest fief that later passed on to me. Sir Eberhard was tall, strong, and handsome. Although his means were always quite limited, in shining armor with a sword at his side and mounted on his splendid charger, he looked as knightly as old Barbarossa himself. He was away much of the time: to serve with the guard of his liege lord, Count Poppo the Elder of Wertheim, or to support (for pay, of course) some other lord who had a dispute with a neighbor—the firm, restraining hand of the emperor could not be omnipresent. With respect to his own affairs, father was not at all quarrelsome and got along well with high and low. But, as much as he loved his family and home, his restless, though happy, spirit could not tolerate the peace and tranquility of Eschenbach for many months at a time. Although by birth an outsider, a Bavarian, he was the pride of the village, and the peasants felt as safe under the protection of the one man as they would have felt with an army to defend them.

On the only occasion, to my knowledge, that he was called upon to justify their trust, his deeds became legend. One day, when I was twelve, a peasant hurried up to our house to report that three horsemen in armor—apparently itinerant mercenaries—were leading away one of his cows. Father was well prepared. While I ran to saddle and fetch his steed, he donned his hauberk, mail stockings, and helmet; buckled on his sword belt; selected a long, sturdy spear; and released his hounds from their pen. In no more than five minutes he was charging out of the gate with a dozen baying dogs in joyous pursuit.

The robbers had gone just a few hundred yards when they heard the commotion and boldly turned to face their lone antagonist. Still they had only their swords, and, since none wanted to be the target of the long spear, they turned away at the last moment and tried to evade the charge. Father quickly overtook one, and the spear threw him over his horse's head. The man was unhurt, but before he could get to his feet, the hounds were upon him and held him down as if he were a beast of prey.

While his companions were hastening to his aid, father wheeled about and charged again. A second robber was felled and seized by the hounds; the third one fled. At my father's command, the peasants led the two captives to an oak beside the road, just outside the village, and hanged them. "Let them dangle there for a time," he said. "Even good, honest men may profit by a reminder of the wages of sin." He was pleased with the wages of righteousness—swords, armor, and two fine steeds—but not quite satisfied. "It's too bad about that last horse," he said to mother later. "I was hoping to get all three."

Mother was quite different from Sir Eberhard. Serious, devout, and patient, she managed the small household—three servant girls, my sister Anna, and me—with quiet efficiency and took care of all commerce with the peasants. She was busy from dawn till dark except for the hour before bedtime when she would tell us stories, both sacred and secular. I don't know where she got them all and suspect that most were her own invention. Her name was Gertrud. She was the daughter of Sir Georg of Abenberg—who, like my father, was a vassal of Count Poppo—and the niece of Abbot Hugo of the Benedictine monastery at Ansbach. As a young girl she had planned to become a nun, but her uncle had dissuaded her. "I am very fond of Gertrud," he once told my father, "but with respect to doctrine, she has always been a free thinker. The Church may eventually adopt some of her beliefs, but not in this century." Perhaps it was due to her influence that certain ideas of mine have been thought unorthodox.

One of mother's stories, about a prince and a fairy queen, especially impressed me and, at my urging, she repeated it quite a few times. Although a little long, it is worth telling, for I think that in some indirect ways it may have influenced my own compositions:

Once upon a time the young prince of a mountainous kingdom was hunting alone with his falcon in an Alpine meadow several miles from his castle. About noon the bright, spring day became overcast and gloomy, so he gave up his sport and set out for home, but a dense fog soon descended and he lost his way. When the fog lifted, he saw that he was riding down through a strange forest. There were many different kinds of trees, but all had large, green leaves and were covered either with blossoms or with fruit—ripe fruit apparently—even though it was only April. The air was warm and fragrant. In the valley below, the fields were brilliant with flowers and low bushes that were covered with shining, red berries. Scattered here and there were cottages with thatched roofs and brightly painted walls; the tables and chairs in front of them showed that the inhabitants spent much of their time in the open.

A few young men and women were walking about, not working, just strolling along in small groups. All had golden hair and yellow garments that were trimmed with other summer colors; they were very handsome. They laughed and sang with clear, melodious voices that differed greatly from those with which the prince was familiar, although the language was German. "Where am I; what country is this?" the prince asked a young maiden.

"It has no proper name," she answered and seemed not at all surprised to see him; "we just call it Our Land."

"And who is your lord?" he inquired.

"We have no lord, but a queen," was the reply. "Her name is Terdelaschoye and she lives in the distant grove yonder." Riding along the paths that crossed the fields, the prince entered the shade of a score of mighty trees and found a small, but elegant, palace with a large lawn in front. At his request, a doorman took him at once to the queen, who was chatting with a group of her friends in the main hall. He had never seen such a lovely creature—indeed there was something unreal about her beauty—and he fell deeply in love at once. The lady, for her part, was greatly impressed by the prince with his coal-black hair; dark, romantic eyes; and grave, sensitive face.

When he explained that he had gotten lost and had wandered into her land unwittingly, she laughed and promised to supply a guide to lead him back to familiar territory. "But I see no need for haste," she added. "Remain with us for a few days; I think you will find your stay enjoyable."

The days stretched into weeks of bowling and dancing on the lawn, of outdoor feasts with fine wines and the many delicious fruits that grew everywhere untended, of the sweetest flute music, and of strange, dream-like recitations about a remote past. Finally the prince could not be persuaded to stay longer, because he knew that his old father, the king, and perhaps the entire land would be grieving for him. "Come with me and be my bride," he told the queen. "Everyone in my country will adore you."

"Gladly," she replied at once. "We shall leave in the morning."

Since there were no horses in the land, the prince's steed had to carry them both up the mountain side and through the thick cloud that still lay on the divide. Although one could not see more than ten feet ahead, the queen directed them surely, and in an hour or so they came down out of the mist to an area with which the prince was familiar. They were soon at his castle, and the land that had been mourning rejoiced. The king was as charmed by the lady as his son had been, and the wedding took place at once.

The country was happier that year than ever before. The

sweet laughter and singing of the queen, the merriment of dances and feasts in the castle or—in fine weather—in the meadow below created a mood of lighthearted good will that spread to all corners of the land. And when the queen gave birth to a beautiful, fair-haired son, there were celebrations in every village.

It was then that the old king died, and, since he was dearly loved by all his subjects, the entire country went into mourning. But while he lay in state in the main hall of the castle, surrounded by weeping and lamenting members of the court, the clear voice of the queen was heard in merry song. Everyone was horrified, and the prince rushed angrily to her chamber to confront her. "What do you mean by this?" he demanded. "Have you no feelings?"

"I am sorry to upset you," she answered calmly. "The song just came out; I couldn't help it. Since I have been here, I have seen people grieve and lament, and I have tried in vain to do so too. I think my joy would be greater and my love stronger if I could be sad, but I can't. It is an emotion that is foreign to those of Our Land."

"You are a monster!" cried the prince in a rage. "And you shall leave this country at once. One of my knights will take you to the mountain heights where I was lost, and you can find your way from there alone and on foot." As soon as a horse was saddled, the queen was carried off.

The prince had no sleep that night as anger struggled with grief—not for the death of his father, but for the loss of his beautiful, joyous wife. In the morning he led a hundred men to the mountain to look for the hidden valley so that he could beg forgiveness and bring her back. They searched everywhere, in every glen, with no success, although there was neither mist on the land nor cloud in the sky. The search continued for two weeks, but in vain. "How wrong I was!" groaned the prince. "We all must act according to our natures—we have no choice—and, despite the one shortcoming, her nature was the most charming I've ever known."

The prince was heartbroken and would have wasted away with sorrow, had it not been for his son. As a baby, he laughed and played throughout his waking hours; as a boy and a youth, he acted as if life were one continuous festival of singing, dancing, and sport; as a man and a king, he made all those around him feel that the world was made for happiness and mirth.

I often thought that my carefree father must have been a descendant of that king. He did much to make my childhood happy; so did its setting. When I was not helping with the housework or father was not teaching me to ride and fence, I played with the peasant children. The dark and tangled forest to the east was a place of mystery that small boys could people with the fairies, elves, and dragons of folklore. Several times I caught a brief glimpse of the dwarf-king Laurin before he could vanish into his magic cloak; the sight of children is much better than that of their elders, who see only what everyone sees. To venture into this forest, even a little ways, was a thrilling experience.

The stream that runs past Eschenbach has a long pool where we skated in winter and swam, fished, and poled a raft in summer. Along the banks were tall maples from whose boughs we could spring into the water, a sport that gave me a reputation for courage that I did not deserve. There was always competition among the boys to see who dared leap from the very highest limbs and, however frightened he might be, the son of Sir Eberhard dared not let himself be outdone by a peasant. To be forced to uphold the honor of his class is a heavy burden for a child, and I often wished that I was a simple peasant who did not need to be brave. It is a wish to which I occasionally returned as a man.

We often had mock battles and dashed about on broom steeds, dealing out vigorous blows with wooden swords. The knight's son was not spared; as in actual warfare, there was little regard for station. But when I went hunting with my bow in the open forest to the north, I went alone. It was then I learned that the killing of hares was restricted to the nobility. "Peasants should not be encouraged to become poachers," said father. "I spare their cattle and they must not kill my game." From twelve on I hunted deer with him, but didn't really enjoy it; the contrast between the beautiful, living creature and the lifeless carcass always saddened me. I said nothing about this to father, who would not have approved of such womanish feelings.

The high points of the year were the May Day and harvest festivals. After attending mass, the entire village ate at tables set up in the open. All sorts of contests followed: foot racing, high jumping, broad jumping, casting a heavy stone, and other tests of skill and strength. Later, old and young joined in lively group dances on the meadow to the music of a fiddler. Sometimes this would be a wandering musician from a different region who would teach us new steps and new songs to sing as we danced. "What a merry life he must have," I thought as a boy, "filled with constant feasting and dancing." And I never ceased to be amazed at how my stately father on these days could spring gaily to the beat, a peasant girl on either hand, and not lose a whit of dignity or respect. He certainly did not resemble the foolish Knight of Reuenthal of whom Sir Neidhart later sang. In some ways the manners of the village are more subtle than those of the court.

The parish priest was a young man with a fine voice; I never heard masses sung more sweetly. He formed a children's choir that often took part in the liturgy and sang hymns at various religious festivals. Who can blame him for choosing Sir Eberhard's son for the solos? Latin seemed much different, more melodious, when it came from my own mouth, and I promised myself that I would learn the language. Alas for the resolves of childhood! I didn't even learn to read and write German until nearly thirty. Still the hymns taught me something about melodies and thus contributed later to the songs that were my first compositions.

Eschenbach was almost my whole world as a child, the single addition being Abenberg. Several times each summer the four of us—Anna riding behind father, I behind mother—would take the river road through the forest to spend a few days there with my grandparents, my uncle and his wife, and their two sons, Albrecht and Diether—one slightly older, the other slightly younger than I. I always looked forward to these trips, not only because of my cousins—of whom I was quite fond—but because the short journey was exciting. As there was little commerce between the two villages, the river road was really little more than a forest trail, that led across three rather steep ravines and two fords. Riding alone in dry weather and on a fresh steed, father could cover the distance in two hours—so he maintained—but it took the four of us twice as long. Since my lust for excitement was more easily satisfied after I grew older, I then communicated with Abenberg usually by messenger.

On my fourteenth birthday Sir Eberhard announced that he had made arrangements for me to serve as a page at Count Poppo's court, where I would learn courtly manners and become acquainted with other youths of my station. I was delighted. Since I had never been more than thirteen miles from home, Wertheim, ninety miles away, seemed almost as remote as China. I knew that the journey itself would be a great adventure. It was 1184, by an auspicious coincidence, the same year that the Hohenstaufen Barbarossa introduced his two older sons, Heinrich and Friedrich, to Europe's heads of state with a knighting festival at Mainz that was attended by fifty thousand nobles and their attendants. We started out on a clear June morning two weeks later. One horse carried father, the other bore me and the baggage: a small tent, provisions for four days, and all of my clothing. My mother and my sister both wept when we departed; the former because I was leaving her for the first time, the latter because she was not going too. But Anna, then twelve, was comforted on being assured that in two or three years she could become a maid-in-waiting of a countess or duchess at some lively court.

I was amazed and thrilled by the strange world beyond: the

great monastery at Ansbach; the castles hanging from the mountain sides near Uffenheim; the wide Main river and the large ships at Ochsenfurt; the busy city of Würzburg with its tall cathedral and mighty fortress; and the wild, dense forest that stretched all the way from Würzburg to Wertheim. No journey in after years was so awe-inspiring. On the fifth day, when we rode up to the count's castle above the town of Wertheim. I felt as if I were entering one of mother's wondrous tales.

As soon as we dismounted, father turned me over to the steward of the castle, said goodbye, and went to report to the count, in whose company he was to leave the following morning for Bamberg. The steward introduced me to four youths, who were my companions for the next few years. At first they called me a backwoodsman, since they had never heard of Eschenbach, but it was good-humored teasing and did not last long. The fact that I was a sturdy lad and somewhat larger than they may have been taken into consideration.

Among other duties, we set up tables in the great hall for the morning and evening meals and served food and drink to the ruling family, the count's guests, and the titled members of his retinue. This brought us into frequent contact with the head cook, a man to whom I became greatly indebted and would never have treated as rudely as his counterpart was by the youthful Rennewart in my Willehalm story. He was a Frenchman. The moment I discovered this, I renounced the mastery of Latin, as a goal, to that of learning French. For, although mother did not know this language, she had said of many of her stories that they came from France. Its speech therefore was the door to the world of romance, and I was determined to enter.

Much of my time was spent with the good cook, who seemed as eager to teach as I was to learn. He had a raucous voice, but he liked to sing and knew many French songs: sacred, profane, and bawdy. I learned them all, even before I understood the words. Once when I was singing one to myself, the countess, Lady Hilde, overheard me and was both surprised and pleased, for she was from the Rhineland and knew French. "Do you know any other songs in that tongue?" she asked.

"Yes, my lady," I replied, "quite a few." The countess thereupon decided that I should give a concert of French songs. I was to teach the melodies to her chamberlain, who played the fiddle, and we were to perform before her friends in two weeks.

The day came and I found myself standing nervously in front of a rather large group of ladies, one of whom was my lady's neighbor, the widely traveled Baroness of Durne, who also knew French. As soon as I began to sing, I felt at ease, for the audience was most receptive. The first three songs were applauded with enthusiasm, but in the middle of the fourth, my lady suddenly stood up and motioned for me to stop. "Tell me, young man," she demanded, "do you know what you are saying?"

"No, countess," I replied timidly. "I have just begun to learn the language."

"Well then, continue," she said and laughed. I did so. Not until I had mastered French did I understand why she and the baroness found some of the songs very amusing. I then learned that grand ladies are not easily shocked.

It was the beginning of my career as an entertainer. Having heard me sing in a language I did not know, the countess concluded that others could do this too, so she decided that the chamberlain and I should be the leaders at a dance. I'll describe what this meant, since the dances of your day may be quite different. We had a singer and a fiddler who was also the dance master. The former sang a stanza of a song and the latter accompanied him while demonstrating the proper dance steps. Then the entire group would repeat the stanza and the steps. This routine was continued throughout the song and the following songs.

The dance went off very well. I had a fine tenor voice—I confess it; the chamberlain was not only an excellent dancer but was also quite inventive; the melodies were new and lovely; and the lords and ladies enjoyed singing in French. The countess had bidden us leave out those songs that had evoked her laughter during my recital. With our reputation thus established, the chamberlain and I led the dancing at court festivities for several years. I added German songs to my repertoire, especially those by a Heinrich of Veldeke, who was at the court of Count Hermann of Thuringia. These were delightful, light-hearted lyrics set to French melodies, and my learning them was a part of a world-shaking conflict.

When Saladin conquered Jerusalem and old Friedrich Barbarossa, king of Germany and emperor of the Holy Roman Empire, decided to have his eldest son, Heinrich, reign in his place while he led a Crusade against the Moslems, his friend Count Hermann of Thuringia invited the lords of all the neighboring lands to Castle Neuenburg on the Unstrut River to discuss their aid to the emperor. Lady Hilde, who would never think of missing such an occasion, accompanied her husband and his retinue with six of her ladies. She also took the chamberlain and me—so that we could provide entertainment along the way and could learn new songs and dances at Count Hermann's court.

The ten-day journey was like an endless parade. We sang to the chamberlain's fiddle while riding along and were guests at the various courts between Wertheim and Neuenberg. Perplexed as to the purpose of the Crusade, I asked Sir Einhart, our count's steward, to explain the matter. I learned that Barbarossa wanted to tear Jerusalem away from the Moslems but did not want to take possession of it, even though its capture would cost many German lives; and also that the emperor had to get there before his two arch-enemies, the kings of England and France, who likewise wished to free the city but not keep it. I was quite embarrassed at being so simple-minded about these logical actions and, fearing to reveal how little we villagers understood such great events, did not broach the subject again.

It was a lively and festive scene that greeted us on the broad field below Castle Neuenburg. At least a hundred large, brightly colored tents were pitched under the trees that lined the river bank; many small groups strolled about while busily discussing all sorts of matters, great and trivial; a dozen knights were displaying the merits of their steeds as they raced back and forth from one end of the field to the other; joyous cries filled the air as we and other late arrivals were welcomed by those who had come earlier. One would have thought that all had gathered there for a tournament or a dance rather than for a council of war. Count Poppo, his wife, and her ladies rode on up to the castle, where they would stay, the rest of us set up camp by the river.

During the following week, the lords spent their mornings and afternoons discussing the amount of gold and troops each was to furnish the emperor, while their retainers amused themselves on the field below with games, contests, and musical performances. A score or more of minstrels, including the chamberlain and me, played and sang to enthusiastic audiences, but the greatest applause was received by Heinrich of Veldeke, a genial Limburger who played the fiddle as he sang his merry songs and demonstrated the dance steps that accompanied them. If I remember rightly, they especially liked these two:

I beg thee, Love, whose yoke I don,
who has captured me as a prize,
that thou mayest hurry my sweetheart on
to better reward my sighs.
For should I fare as doth the swan,
who sings his melody and dies,
I would pay too much for the joy I've won.

Tristan, not from his desire,
served the queen with true devotion,
subject to a lover's fire
less than to a magic potion.
Therefore should my lady thank
me, for though I never drank
such a brew, my heart's emotion
equals that from witch's wine.
Thing of beauty, truth and duty,

grant that I be thine
and that thou be mine.

In the evenings all who could crowd into the great hall listened to Heinrich read from his poem about the Trojan Aeneas. Thrilled by the tale, I determined then and there that some day I too would compose a romance, but one with a more sensitive hero. I was always an incurable romantic.

Despite the splendid August weather, our company was quite subdued during the journey home. The chamberlain and I went over the many new songs we had learned and most of the others sang the verses after me, but their gaiety was rather forced. At the urging of Hermann, who was representing the emperor, Count Poppo had agreed to furnish a large number of troops for the Crusade, and everyone was wondering who the conscripts would be. However reasonable it might seem for Barbarossa to get to Jerusalem before the French and the English, there appeared to be little eagerness to accompany him. I was a little surprised, for I had heard a wandering minstrel at Wertheim recite the poem about Emperor Karl and Roland and had assumed that everyone but I would consider it a rare privilege to take part in a Crusade. Still I was not concerned, for I did not think father would be chosen—there was no one else to manage our fief at Eschenbach—and it did not occur to me that I myself might be sent.

When we returned to Wertheim, I became the steward's assistant and was no longer addressed by the servants as "Wolf" but as "Squire Wolfram." I was overwhelmed by this giant step upward and thought it only a matter of time until I became the chief adviser of the count. But fate ordained that I was not to be a polished courtier but a rustic, unkempt householder such as Sir Hartmann of Aue describes in his Iwein romance.

Soon after the news of Barbarossa's Crusade had spread abroad, Sir Eberhard appeared at Wertheim with two chargers and a packhorse bearing a two-year supply of everything an experienced campaigner would need except food. He came for me at once and took me with him to see the count. "I have come to join your Crusaders," said father, "and I would like to have you recognize my son here as the right lord of Eschenbach during my absence. Although only eighteen, he is as large and strong as a man and, while here at your court, has doubtless learned what a vassal needs to know,"

"He'll do very well," replied Count Poppo, "and you shall lead my company. It must be ready to join the emperor in Regensburg before the first of May." That was all; the old count was a man of few words. A week later I set out for home. Wearing the coat of mail, helmet, and sword that father had brought me, I felt very much a knight but also a little frightened, for I had never before traveled alone. It had not been easy to leave my friends—the other youths, the chamberlain, and the old French cook—and I nearly wept when I said goodbye to my light-hearted father, who at the moment appeared much more serious than usual. I followed the roads we had taken years before—through Würzburg, Ochsenfurt, Uffenheim, and Ansbach—and was surprised at how different everything appeared: still large and splendid, but no longer wondrous. One loses much with childhood.

Two important tasks awaited me on my return: carrying out the promise made to my sister and meeting with the village elders. The first was much easier than I had anticipated because mother had already made the necessary arrangements through her uncle, the abbot. As the head of a wealthy and influential monastery, it had been easy for him to persuade the count of the principality of Ansbach to invite his grandniece and godchild to become a maid-in-waiting at the count's court, that was in the city of Ansbach.

When I arrived in Eschenbach, our entire household was busily sewing, so that Anna would be properly attired. Two weeks later I accompanied her to the monastery and placed her in the care of the abbot. Mother bore up very well under this parting, for Ansbach was less than three hours away and she could expect to see her daughter often. When I told Abbot Hugo about my singing for dances, he urged me to return as soon as my affairs were in order and perform for the monks; one of them, Brother Andrew, played the fiddle and could quickly learn the melodies. "But uncle," I said, "I only know the love songs one sings for dances."

"I thought as much," he replied. "But, although not good dancers, we Benedictines are not averse to hearing or singing about a love that we deny ourselves."

The second task worried me greatly, for I knew that the peasants would compare me with the incomparable Sir Eberhard and that my authority would therefore suffer greatly. My wise mother knew the answer. "Speak always in the name of your father," she said, "and when they look at you, they will see him." It was very effective. I told the assembled elders that their lord, the famous warrior who was now the leader of the count's army, had instructed me to see that the order he had established was maintained and to settle all disputes as he would have settled them.

My first test came two months later. Hans, a single youth of nineteen, and Gregor, married and the father of three young children, got into a fight and Gregor was killed. A careful questioning of the villagers revealed that the two had often quarreled before, but nobody knew who had struck the first blow on this occasion. Several men had seen the end of the struggle and they agreed that the death was largely an accident: Gregor had been thrown to the ground and his head had struck a large rock. I gave orders that Hans be tied up for the night and said that I would render a judgment the following morning.

What was to be done? The matter was indeed serious. A man had died, leaving three orphans and a widow who would not be able to manage her fields and probably could not find another husband because of her children and her sharp tongue. Yet how could I tell which man was really at fault? Perhaps Hans was only defending himself. Finally I asked mother for advice. "Sir Eberhard was never as concerned about guilt or innocence," she said, "as with practical solutions to immediate problems."

Shortly after daybreak I summoned the village elders and ordered that the prisoner be brought before me for sentencing. "You have deprived a man of his life, a woman of her husband, and three children of a father. You will replace him by marrying his widow and raising his children as your own. If you run away, you will be outlawed and hanged as soon as you are caught." The peasants were well satisfied with the judgment. Even Hans thought it preferable to being hanged at once, as he had feared. Actually the marriage turned out rather well, for Hans's wife never felt sure that he would stay and therefore gave him better treatment than her first husband had had.

It was about this time that I returned to Ansbach to accept the abbot's invitation to sing at the monastery. I arrived about noon and went over the songs for several hours with Brother Andrew. He was a jovial fellow—truly a master with the fiddle—who learned the melodies very quickly. We practiced for several hours and presented them after the evening meal. The monks were delighted and repeated the stanzas of the love songs after me with much greater enthusiasm than I had expected of those sworn to celibacy. This, my first performance with Brother Andrew, was followed by many others during the next forty-five years, at the monastery and at village festivals in Eschenbach. The latter occasions enabled me to step somewhat out of my father's shadow, for his voice was more like a raven's than a nightingale's.

After his death I also distinguished myself from Sir Eberhard in another way, one of which he would not have approved: I formed something of a partnership with the peasants. Wanting to be able to get away from Eschenbach now and then, I asked the priest for suggestions as to how the village could be so organized as to make it easy for my mother to direct its affairs in my absence. "I think you should appoint a forceful and respected peasant to represent the village with you or your mother," he said. "He could also see that your or her orders were carried out and even help in the defense of the village from robbers."

"And how much should I pay this man?" I asked. "You know that our means are limited."

"Oh, you wouldn't need to pay him anything," replied the good father. "Just give him a title. Call him 'meyer,' that comes from the Latin word meaning one who is greater than others."

"But it doesn't seem fair to me," I protested, "to pay a man for his services with nothing but a word."

"My dear sir," replied the priest, "you vastly underrate the importance of a word. Princes have wasted their fortunes and fought bloody wars to be called 'King of the Germans' or 'Emperor of the Holy Roman Empire,' even though no monetary reward accompanies either title. And remember what the Scripture says: 'In the beginning was the word.' As a singer, you should have a higher regard for the tools of the trade."

I agreed to try it. Calling all of the heads of families together, I appointed one of them "meyer," with the responsibility to act as spokesman for the villagers and to assist me or, in my absence, my mother in defense of the community and in the conduct of village affairs. The recipient of the title was delighted and said nothing about a more substantial recompense for his services. I resolved to give considerable thought to this reaction when time permitted.

A little more than a year after my return to Eschenbach, I decided to ride to Wertheim to pay my respects to the count, learn what I could about father, and visit my friends. Sir Poppo was well satisfied with my stewardship, but he had little news of Barbarossa's army. My former companions, especially the cook and the chamberlain, were happy to see me, and the countess at once arranged for the latter and me to perform at a dance. While we were preparing for it, the chamberlain taught me several new songs that he had heard recently. From France had come a new kind of love song that told of the sad parting of secret lovers after a night together. I was so excited by the dramatic possibilities of the situation that I composed one myself, both the lyrics and the tune. Not intended for dancing, it goes like this:

Watchman:

Dawn strikes its claws
through massive clouds and mounts in flight.
It rises with relentless power
and with it draws
the graying shadows of the night.
I see the day, which at this hour
will steal the pleasure of the man
whom I admitted fearfully.
I'll get him out now if I can;

his stately bearing must have blinded me.

Lady:

The song you sing,
O watchman, takes my joy away
and makes more grievous my lament.
The news you bring
each morning at the break of day
gives only sorrow and discontent.
Such words I do not care to hear,
so hold your tongue and let us be,
and I'll reward you, never fear,
if my dear love remains a while with me.

Watchman:

He still must go,
sweet lady, say goodbye, that he
may leave as promptly as he came,
and later show
his love for you more stealthily,
preserve his honor and his good name.
He trusted in my faithfulness
to get him safely forth from here;
the night has past when your caress
and kisses bought my aid to bring him near.

Lady:

Sing what you will,
O watchman, sing, but let him stay,
who brought his love and here found mine.
Your rough words fill
us always with intense dismay.
Before the morning star can shine
upon this knight who visits me,
while still no rays of sunshine part
the night, you make him rise and flee
from my bare arms, but never from my heart.

Poet:

But still the clear
bright rays the sun cast overhead
and the warning watchman's rude request
caused her to fear
for the gallant knight who shared her bed:

she pressed him closely to her breast.
And yet the knight was strong and brave
despite the watchman's song above;
their warm and tender parting gave
them kisses (and much more) as spoils of love.

The chamberlain, who could sing while he played, agreed to take the role of the watchman; his voice was a little rough, but his pitch was true. When we asked the countess to sing the lady's verses, she was both pleased and flattered and at once consented; although she had a small voice, it was clear and carried well. I took the part of the poet. The performance was a great success: the listeners insisted that it be repeated several times, and they sang along with much zest during the final performance. It was so well received that, at a single stroke, I won a reputation as a poet, which changed the course of my life. For the little song led to the poems about Parzival and Willehalm. Great oaks from little acorns grow.

Just before I was to set out for home, the startling news arrived at the court that the emperor was dead. Hoping to get some report about father, I delayed my return and, sure enough, a week later a messenger arrived with a letter from him to the count. After it had been read to Sir Poppo, he gave it to me as a memento of a father who might never return. I kept the letter all my life. It read as follows:

"Renowned Count Poppo of Wertheim! I have sad news: the emperor is dead, his mighty army is in disarray, and most of the survivors, including the bearer of this message, are returning in separate groups to Germany. Since I shall remain here, the letter will be my report on the Crusade that you have supported. As you are doubtless aware, Barbarossa took the land route through Hungary, Serbia, and Greece. Since we were constantly harassed in Greece by troops of its emperor, Barbarossa seized his city of Adrianopel and threatened to destroy it. We were then given free passage. Our army crossed over the straits at Gallipoli and fought its way with many losses to Ikonion, where we won two great battles over the superior forces of its sultan. Turning south, we crossed the Taurus Mountains. As it was midday when we reached the Salef River, the army stopped there for an hour's rest, and old Barbarossa decided to bathe in its wild waters. No one could dissuade him. I did not see it myself, but I was told that he was seized by a merman, drawn under, and drowned. It was our only encounter with the monstrous men and beasts that, according to the minstrel's tales, Alexander the Great met with in this region.

"You will understand our dilemma. Most of the great lords feel that their allegiance was to the emperor, who is dead, rather than to the Crusade, and they intend to go to the coastal towns still under Christian control, sail for Italy, and find their way home from there. I have left your knights free to make their own decisions, but I shall go with the emperor's son, Duke Friedrich of Swabia, who will lead three hundred of us on to Jerusalem. The English Richard the Lion-hearted should arrive soon to help us. Your loyal vassal, Sir Eberhard of Eschenbach."

I hurried home to tell mother of the emperor's death and father's decision. "Three hundred men against the countless hordes of Saladin!" she cried. "Oh the folly of those who know no fear! He will never come back." It was only the second time that I had seen her weep. She was right. Two years later we learned that King Richard had come too late and that Duke Friedrich with all of his men had died in the battle for Jerusalem.

In the meantime my chief concern was getting my sister married. At the court of the Count of Ansbach she and a young lord of Lichtenau had become attracted to each other, and the latter's father, Baron Siegfried, had expressed his willingness to have Anna as his daughter-in-law if she could bring with her a proper dowry. That was the problem, for I knew that what he would consider suitable would be far beyond our modest means. Nevertheless I decided to go to Ansbach and talk with Abbot Hugo, who had favored the union. "I'm afraid it is out of the question," I told him. "Mother and I live frugally and are getting along quite well, but we are not wealthy and could never meet the baron's expectations."

"I think I can help you," he replied. "The monastery has a forest that he would like. Indeed, he thinks it really should be his and would be delighted to accept it in place of a dowry."

"But how could you give it to him?" I objected. "The forest is not yours; it belongs to the monastery."

"I'm inclined to doubt it," said the abbot, "and have thought for some time that its ownership should be reexamined. This seems to be a good time to do so. My predecessor, Abbot Johann, was on occasion a bit overzealous in advancing the fortunes of the monastery. On the death of Sir Diepold, the grandfather of the present baron of Lichtenau, his heirs were shown a document in which he deeded the forest to the monastery. They were astonished, because he had never been very pious, but there it stood on good parchment with his signature.

"I was just a youth then—this was thirty years ago—but I too was surprised, for I knew the baron slightly and had no idea that he was learned enough to write his name. Later, after becoming abbot, I searched through the archives and found the document. If I may say so, I am an expert on handwriting, and I am sure that the same hand penned both the signature and the Latin text. Baron Diepold certainly knew no Latin. Since then I have waited for the proper moment to return the forest to its true owner.

"As you say, I cannot give what is not mine, and I am reluctant to confess that it was stolen from the baron's family. But while we are discussing the marriage, I'll bring up the matter of the forest. I'll say that the grandfather might have been sick and not quite in his right mind when he signed the deed, and I'll imply that the monastery might be persuaded to give up the forest. Then he'll gladly accept whatever dowry you propose. Each will benefit: your sister will be well married, the baron will get his forest, and my conscience will be clear."

Everything happened as the kindly old abbot predicted, and my weighty problem was solved. I have often marveled at how Providence rewards the humble leaders of the Church and those whom it favors.

Two years passed, during which I made my annual journeys to Wertheim to report to the count and to learn from the chamberlain the new songs that had been sung there. Three love lyrics had been composed by Emperor Heinrich himself. When we performed them for the countess and her friends, she was so kind as to say that, while they were pretty, they were not as good as mine. I was flattered, of course. To be superior to the emperor is no small achievement whatever the endeavor. "I am surprised that he made the verses in German," she continued. "He is also king of Italy, you know, and spends most of his time there. I wonder who the ladylove of his songs is; it is certainly not his wife.

"And speaking of wives," said the countess, "one of my maidens-in-waiting, Anna of Lengfurt, is now of marriageable age and would rather remain here than go back to her parents. Why don't you marry her—I think it could be arranged—and return to your position as assistant to the steward? You could find someone to manage your fief."

I thanked her for her interest in me and promised to discuss the matter with my kinsmen. At first the proposal seemed very appealing. I hardly knew Anna, but she was attractive, and so was the prospect of having Wertheim as a permanent residence. After all, life in Eschenbach might get a little boring. I thought of nothing else on the way home. And the closer I got to Eschenbach, the more I wondered whether I really wanted to leave it. I decided to stop at the Ansbach monastery and talk with Abbot Hugo.

It was mid-afternoon when I rang the bell and asked to speak with the abbot. He was delighted to see me. "You must stay over night and sing for us after vespers," he said. "I'll get Brother Andrew, and you can start rehearsing at once."

"Very well," I replied, "but I have come to get your advice concerning a personal problem."

"And you shall have it," he promised, "this evening after

you have earned it with a fine performance. I'll go find our fiddler. There is no time to waste."

Andrew and I did very well, I confess it, and we richly deserved the applause we received. The monks were delighted with the new songs and were especially interested in those by young Heinrich. "It's too bad that he was destined to be an emperor," said one, "with a little more practice he could be a great poet and composer."

When the group dispersed, I told the abbot what the countess had said. "I could advise you better if I knew you better," he responded, "but I can say that your father, who was more restless than I believe you to be, had the same choice. Whether it be a village or a castle, a place has only one master, and he decided that he would rather be the lord of Eschenbach than a servant at Wertheim. Moreover there is another reason to stay here. The emperor has to deal with revolts in Italy and with the insurrection of Duke Heinrich the Lion of Saxony. If the pope should excommunicate the emperor, as he has threatened to do, the forces of Duke Heinrich could be strong enough to engulf all Germany in fratricidal war. Eschenbach might well escape it, but not Wertheim. Were I to counsel you, I would say: marry someone from this region, compose your songs in your spare time, and come here to sing them."

I left the following morning and arrived at Eschenbach before noon. "Something terrible has happened," said mother as soon as I entered the house. "Your cousin Diether has died. His horse stumbled and fell on him. Now his pretty, young wife is a widow and his baby daughter is an orphan. That would be a good match for you. I mentioned the possibility to your uncle who approved and said that she would bring with her all the land that he had given his son." Thus do the gods determine our fate. After three months of mourning, we were married; my Katharina was a loyal and loving wife for forty-three summers and as many winters.

The next few years were uneventful and, except for the trips to Wertheim, my travels were restricted to Ansbach and Abenberg. I often thought about the abbot's dire predictions and, since he somehow managed to keep well informed about German and Empire matters, I visited him rather frequently just to hear the latest news. Sometimes we would talk all night about the individual German princes and the role each might play in the power struggle for control of Germany and the Empire. Again and again Hugo would bring up Pope Innocence, who, he thought, was always working behind the scenes to turn German against German for his own advantage.

My new status as head of a family and my responsibility for the peasants made me feel obliged to keep informed about important events. "I wish to serve Eschenbach," I once told the abbot "as well as Heinrich serves the Empire." Such is the idealism of youth! When I learned that Duke Leopold of Austria had captured the English King Richard the Lion-Hearted, a strong supporter of Duke Heinrich, and had turned him over to the emperor, I supposed that the danger to Germany was over. And, sure enough, to gain freedom for Richard, the duke yielded to Heinrich—according to the abbot's sources—and the peace was confirmed by the marriage of the former's son to the latter's cousin. Secure at home, the emperor now planned to take over Greece and, using it as a base, conquer the Orient. At least this was the rumor among Churchmen.

News of the death of the emperor, leaving his three-year-old son as his heir apparent, was a shock to me but it did not seem ominous, for Heinrich's brother, Philip of Swabia, who was to serve as regent, was both wise and strong. So said Hugo, who had known him when the duke was bishop of Würzburg. Yet the abbot declared that Duke Heinrich's ambitious son, Otto of Braunschweig, would never miss this opportunity to retake the lands his father had lost and become king of Germany. It seemed a poor prophesy at first, for, although the German princes refused to have the child as king, the majority did award the crown to Philip, which was welcome news. But soon afterward we heard that a group of northern princes had not recognized the election as valid and had chosen Otto instead, an action that Philip was apparently ignoring. Then one day the abbey was shaken by the report that the pope had supported Otto's claim. "Philip must attack now or he will be lost!" exclaimed Hugo.

Two years after Innocence's intervention, I changed from a spectator to an actor in the long Welf-Hohenstaufen drama. A messenger arrived with a summons from Count Poppo, and a fortnight later I was one of about forty knights that he put at King Philip's disposal. Riding to Würzburg, our company joined the main army or, to be exact—a virtue that chroniclers seldom possess—the main armies: one commanded by the king, the other by the margrave of Meissen. There were some five hundred knights in all. We then moved northward to reach a settlement, either peaceful or military, with Otto.

Our spirits were high. It was like an immense parade, with a vanguard of trumpeters followed by richly attired knights riding four abreast under colorful banners. Most were young men like myself, trying to conceal their excitement as they approached a possible conflict in which they would show for the first time how well they had mastered the skills that they had spent much of their youth learning. After the evening meal, those not on watch sat around campfires, hearing tales of great valor and singing battle songs. Only the grizzled veterans of earlier campaigns were silent and thoughtful.

We encountered the enemy just beyond Gotha. Since our outriders had given us ample warning, the attack on us was not a surprise, but it soon became clear that neither king nor margrave had expected such a mighty host. Otto had gained allies: we faced the combined forces of Saxony, Thuringia, and Bohemia. As soon as he realized that we were far outnumbered, Philip chose the only course that could save us: we had to reach Erfurt some fifteen miles way. Therefore our entire army charged the enemy troops that stood between us and the town and broke through their lines. From then on the battle consisted of a spirited rear-guard action to cover our flight.

Fortunately for us, Count Hermann of Thuringia had not only concealed his change in loyalty from Philip, but also from the people of Erfurt, who, seeing the king's banner, left the gates open. Quickly taking control of them, we were able to hold off the enemy until our entire force was inside. I can look back on my own deeds that day with considerable satisfaction; had he seen me, Sir Eberhard might not have been greatly impressed, but he would not have been embarrassed. Nevertheless, having once proven my courage, I have never been much inclined to make a habit of it.

There are few places in Germany that are so easy to defend as Erfurt. With high walls and almost encircled by the two arms of the Gera River, the place is a fortress that we could have held against all of Europe. Moreover, Hermann seemed reluctant to break down the walls of his own town, for no catapults were employed. After a few vain attempts to storm the walls, the enemy settled down to a long siege in hope of starving us into submission. It was a prospect that was not at all pleasing to those of us who liked to eat regularly, but Philip declared that, although our food had to be carefully rationed, help would no doubt come within a few months. Fortunately we had been able to bring the supply wagons with us during our hurried retreat.

After observing the enemy posts for a week, Philip chose two routes by which a clever and swift runner might be able to escape and he selected two men who were familiar with the region. They would have to swim the river, of course, for the passage by land would be too carefully guarded. Avoiding all roads, they were to go cross-country to Meiningen, the bishop of which was a close friend of the king, and get fast horses to take them to Bavaria and Swabia, where an army would be mustered to come to our aid. I knew nothing of this at the time, but talked with one of the messengers later. "I left on a dark, stormy night," he said, "when everyone was under cover and nobody could see any further than a yard or two. I reached Meiningen in three days: wet, cold, and exhausted. After a day's rest I left with dry clothes, provisions, and two fast horses. The remainder of the journey was easy."

At first the citizens of Erfurt seemed rather honored by the presence of such a famous guest—although he would have been more welcome if his entourage had been smaller—and appeared quite unpartisan with respect to the struggle for the crown. But when it was clear that we would be staying for some time and that eventually they would have to share their supplies with our troops, the good burghers came forward with various helpful suggestions: our release might be arranged by means of a ransom; Philip could abdicate in favor of Otto; we might burst through their lines in the middle of the night and flee; and others even less promising.

The siege had lasted for more than four months and we were eating just one meal a day when we saw the enemy troops move away from the river banks and down the road toward Gotha, leaving only those in front of the main gates. Soon afterwards we heard the faint sound of trumpets in the direction of Gotha and knew that help had come. The king picked a hundred knights who were to stay inside the walls and defend them. The others were to mount and follow him as soon as our reinforcements came into view. "There they are!" cried a lookout from the church tower. "I can see the Swabian banner." The three gates were thrown open and four hundred knights dashed out, swept through the enemy troops that had been left behind, and raced off to attack the rear of the Saxon, Thuringian, and Bohemian forces.

The battle raged furiously throughout the afternoon. But before evening it was clear that ours was the superior force. The Saxons retreated northward, the Thuringians westward to Eisenach, and the Bohemians fled east toward their homeland. On the following day Hermann sent a message, renouncing his support of Otto and pledging loyalty to Philip. Since the count had many friends among the lords of the region, the king thought it best to forgive the attack and the siege. Remembering the months of short rations, I would have been less generous. I set out for home at once, for I was concerned about the welfare of my family and knew that my wife and my mother would be worried about me. I found both our household and the village in good shape and quite unaware of the historical importance of the victory to which I had contributed.

I believe that I am remembered less as the author of verse romances than as a character in the dramatic poem known as "The Battle of the Singers at Wartburg Castle." Since none of the different versions that I heard gives an accurate account of the episode on which the work is based, it might be well to tell the story of a participant, myself.

About a year after Philip of Swabia and Count Hermann made peace, the latter sent out messengers in all direction to invite the powerful lords of Saxony, Thuringia, and Franconia to a great festival at his Wartburg Castle—perhaps he sought to regain by extravagant hospitality the standing he had lost by his wavering politics. Because of his reputation as a patron of song, poet-composers came from near and far to provide entertainment for the many distinguished guests. The renowned Reinmar of Hagenau and the incomparable Walther of Vogelweide traveled there all the way from Vienna, and the obscure Knight of Eschenbach was summoned by Lady Hilde—who was always eager to increase his repertoire—to join the retainers who would accompany her and the count to Wartburg.

There had not been a celebration like this since Barbarossa's sons were knighted. But I'll omit the description of the many contests, the dancing, the tournament, and the feasting and proceed at once to the mortal combat of the singers. On the last night of the merry-making, the lords and ladies were gathered in the great hall to listen to the singers when a young man, dressed from head to foot in bright red silk rushed in and cried loudly: "I am Heinrich of Ofterdingen and I ask a boon of the worthy Count Hermann."

"What do you want?" asked the count astonished.

"I am the greatest of singers," was the reply, "and I wish to prove it in strife with those here. I shall sing a eulogy of Duke Leopold of Austria and Styria and shall forfeit my head if they can prove in their songs that there are three other princes who are so excellent in every way as he. Let them pay the same price should they fail." There was a long pause. Then, one after the other, his challenge was accepted by Reinmar, Walther, a certain Biterolf, the count's secretary (who was called "the Virtuous Scribe"), and lastly a most reluctant Wolfram.

"So be it!" exclaimed Hermann. "Clear a space in the middle of the hall for the contestants. You listeners shall be the judges and shall cry out the verdict, which my executioner Stempfel, standing by the singers, will carry out at once."

My companions and I in turn then sang our extravagant eulogies in the most lyrical and convincing fashion we could manage, for our lives were at stake. We all began by praising Count Hermann in the highest terms; we couldn't lose here. To him Walther added King Philip of France, and Biterolf extolled the Count of Henneberg as the third peer of the Austrian monarch. Yet they do not call Leopold "the Glorious" without cause, and our opponent praised his many virtues eloquently with excellent verses and a fine tenor voice. To me the outcome seemed in doubt. But when the stranger of Ofterdingen ended his song, Walther asked him: "Would you then compare your duke to the sun?"

"Indeed I would!" cried Heinrich, "for he outshines all else."

"Then he is not the equal of Count Hermann," declared

Walther, "because he is the Day, that is brighter than sun, moon, and all the stars together."

I personally was not greatly impressed by my companion's wit, but the audience was, and with a mighty roar it proclaimed us the victors. Frightened, our opponent dashed through the crowd and, throwing himself at the feet of the countess of Thuringia, begged for his life. Despite the loud objections of the singers who had risked their heads, she interceded for him with her husband, and Heinrich was saved. Thereupon he quickly regained his composure and addressed the count with a second request. "My lord," said Heinrich, "with me is a Master Klingsor of Hungary who is ready to wager his life against that of the wisest of your singers. He wants to test his adversary's knowledge with ten pious riddles that a shrewd Christian should be able to solve."

"I accept the challenge," said the count. "Sir Wolfram here will represent us."

"But, my lord," I protested, "I am no scholar. I can't read."

"No matter," he declared. "Lady Hilde praises your quick wit and says that you even know French. Moreover you are more pious than most. I'm sure you will do well."

A messenger was sent, and the Hungarian soon appeared. A rather short man with a thick, black beard, he wore a long, blue robe that was decorated with many bright stars; a tall, pointed hat came down over his forehead and rested on his heavy eyebrows. The two of us took our places in the center of the hall, and the contest began. After all these years I can't recall the verse in which the riddles were presented, but I can give some of them in prose.

"A father wakes a sleeping child to save it from drowning," sang Klingsor. "What does this mean?"

I was greatly relieved for the moment, because the parish priest of my childhood had often used this parable. "The child is mankind, whom God chastises in order to save," I sang solemnly and with confidence.

After a moment of surprised silence, the master gave the second riddle: "What is like a king's daughter who is married to a rude, coarse man?"

I knew this also from my blessed priest. "The human soul," I responded.

Klingsor was beginning to show concern. "What tree sends its roots to the bottom of hell and its top to the throne of God?" he asked.

Once more the priest's sermons saved me. "The cross of Christ," I replied.

"Who is the young bird that leaves the nest and, soaring high above its father, brings grief and pain upon itself and its brothers and sisters?" demanded Klingsor somewhat fearfully.

"Who but Lucifer," I answered boldly. So it was with the rest of the riddles. I had heard them all. When I solved the tenth one, the Hungarian screamed loudly and, before anyone could stop him, ran swiftly from the hall.

At the door his pursuers were confronted by a very tall man in black, whose piercing eyes and fierce countenance would have cowed a raging lion. "Go back!" he ordered. "I, Nasion, have some things to ask this wise man of yours." Striding to the middle of the hall, he posed a series of questions on the sun, moon, stars, and other matters of astronomy, to all of which I happened to know the answer. At last, tiring of the trial, I drew forth a small crucifix that hung inside my coat and, holding it before me, approached my demonic inquisitor. He retreated to the door in terror, then turned and fled into the darkness. All those in the hall, who had looked on in amazed silence, now burst into applause.

These were the events on which the versions of "The Battle of the Singers" was based. But there was more to it that, by the order of Count Hermann, was kept secret from his many guests. The count had planned the entire episode: Heinrich, Klingsor, and Nasion were servants of the count in disguise, and all their riddles and questions had been prepared by Reinmar, Walther, and me. We were the authors of the song's original and best version, that was never written down. I had been included with the two famous poets because Countess Hilde had praised my compositions. The three of us had drawn lots to see who would solve Klingsor's riddles and answer Nasion's questions and I had won, But I had won much more than the major role in a play. Although quite undeserving, I had gained a reputation for wisdom that led directly to my career as an epic poet.

For most of the way back to Wertheim, Count Poppo's company rode with that of Baron Rupert of Durne, who had traveled widely in the service of Emperor Heinrich and had many connections in France. On a recent journey there he had obtained a manuscript that contained an exciting Arthurian tale, and it occurred to him that his neighbor's vassal would be just the one to put it into German verse. I agreed to come to his castle and do so in the late fall when I would have little to occupy me in Eschenbach. "It will take only a few weeks," I thought and had no idea of the years of labor ahead.

Castle Wildenberg and Parzival

The harvest festival at Eschenbach that year was one of the most enjoyable that I have known. The crops had been abundant, the weather was splendid, and everyone in the village was in the mood for a week of contests, games, feasting, singing, and dancing. Brother Andrew came down from Ansbach to join me, and the two of us kept the villagers springing about merrily on the river meadow for two hours every day. A week later I set out for Baron Rupert's Castle Wildenberg in the Desolate Forest.

On the homeward journey from Wartburg the baron had told us the story of the building of his castle by a forefather over two centuries earlier:

At that time the great forest was the home of a mighty water sprite called Tarn who was said to dwell in an underground cavern that was entered by way of a certain deep pool in the Mudau River. Tarn considered the entire forest his private realm and, while he allowed travelers to pass through, he would not permit anyone to build there or fell a single tree. Woodcutters and settlers perished mysteriously and their bodies were borne from the forest by the river. From time to time people claimed to have gotten a brief glimpse of Tarn, but they gave widely differing descriptions of his appearance. Some said that he looked like a very tall man with long, white hair and a white beard that reached to his knees; others maintained that he resembled a waterfall more than a human being, one that moved about and had neither source nor basin.

Emperor Otto, called "the Great," gave the forest to the baron's distant ancestor, a nobleman named Werner. He was a man of great courage and stubbornness who did not intend to let the sprite keep him from his new fief. He brought in a large crew of masons and carpenters who, quarrying stone and felling trees for timber, began at once to construct a fine castle on the heights above the river. The men were told to stay together and keep weapons handy; no one was to wander off by himself. For a while everything went well and the lord began to doubt the very existence of the sprite.

The outer walls of the castle were almost finished when a new spring appeared further up the mountain, and its water, flowing directly against the castle, threatened to undermine its foundations. The workers hurriedly dug a channel that turned the stream aside, but they had hardly finished when another, larger, spring bubbled up and sent its current against the castle. The masons and carpenters now had to halt construction for several months in order to dig a deep moat to catch all the water that flowed down the mountain. As soon as it was finished, all the springs on the mountain stopped flowing, and water for drinking and for mortar had to be carried up from the river, a thousand feet below.

"It would be useless to dig a well!" exclaimed Werner. "And no one wants to live in a castle that has no water. I must talk with that water sprite."

"I'll pick a dozen good men and we can begin searching for him at once." said his steward.

"No, fourteen men would never find him," answered the baron. "I'll go alone."

"But sir, he hates you, and no one has ever withstood him," objected the steward.

"I'll take the chance," declared Werner. "Otherwise I'd just have to leave this splendid forest. I'll start looking tomorrow."

Early the following morning the baron went down to the river, walked along the bank, and shouted at each pool: "Ho, Tarn! I, Baron Werner, would talk with you." After about an hour he saw a waterfall suddenly appear on the opposite bank. Then, as he watched, it gradually turned into a creature, perhaps seven feet tall, that looked like a man except for ears that resembled those of a deer. It wore a green tunic woven from rushes and had a long, white beard.

"And what do you, who has felled my trees and quarried my stone, have to say before you die?" demanded Tarn.

"That you should be reasonable," replied the baron. "There are settlements on all sides of this great forest, and soon men will be crowding in from north, south, east, and west. Not even a mighty water sprite can stop them unaided. You need an ally. If you let me finish my castle and live here in peace, I swear that I'll never again harm a tree or a stone of the forest and that I'll prevent all others from doing so."

"Suppose I believe you," said Tarn. "You will live only thirty or forty years longer; what about your sons, grandsons, and those who follow?"

"The vow shall be handed down to them," declared Werner. "No one will ever inherit the castle who does not swear to spare and defend every tree and stone of the forest."

"And I shall swear that, if any of you breaks his word, the castle and all its inhabitants shall be destroyed," said the sprite.

"Agreed!" cried the baron and watched as the figure on the other bank slowly changed into a waterfall and flowed into the river.

"Is the water sprite still there?" I asked Sir Rupert. "Have you seen him?"

"No, and neither had my father," he replied. "But there has been no reason for anyone to see him. Before Sir Werner came, he sometimes showed himself in order to frighten away those who might harm his forest. Since then there has been no need for this because we all have kept our ancestor's vow. Like those before me, I have sworn to spare and protect every tree and stone, and I shall keep my word. The water sprite won two hundred years of peace and contentment through the pact; the forest has not changed since then. I don't think he is gone. During my lifetime the regions around us have had three very dry years, serious droughts, but the forest, especially the spring that supplies the castle, was not affected. Somehow he kept us in water."

I stopped at Wertheim—to see my friends and pay my respects to the count and countess—and started out very early the next morning so that I would not have to spend the night in a strange, deserted region. The road ended at the edge of the forest. From here on there was only a narrow path that wound its way carefully around trees and thickets as it climbed the mountain side and descended to the valley of the Mudau. I had never seen such a dark and ancient forest. The crowns of mighty trees formed a dense canopy high above; other giants lay scattered here and there where old age or storms had felled them. I felt as if I had been transported back in time to a distant, primeval age. As I rode south along the river bank, I watched intently in hope of catching a glimpse of Tarn and I did see several falls as mountain streams dropped into the Mudau, but apparently they were no more than they seemed. It was evening when the path turned up the mountain side and brought me to the foot of the high cliff at the top of which Wildenberg rests.

The following day I was introduced to Karl, the baron's scribe, who was to be my companion for many months. "How did Sir Rupert happen to get this manuscript?" I asked when Karl showed it to me.

"While in France on a mission for Emperor Heinrich," answered the old scribe, "he visited Sir Maurice of Craon, a poet and collector of manuscripts of French verse, who read to him selections from an Arthurian romance in his library. Sir Rupert was so charmed by the work that, when he departed, he directed me to stay behind and copy it for him. The two months I was there were enlivened by a rather amusing scandal in which Sir

Maurice was involved. He was a very romantic person and not only composed chivalric love songs, but was also inclined to live them.

"He chose the wife of his neighbor, Viscount Richard de Beaumont, to be his ladylove and served her as her loyal knight by performing all sorts of romantic feats. The most fantastic was a journey he took in what appeared to be a viking ship that he ordered built on a large wagon. It had sail, rudder, oarsmen, and cloth sides that hung from the gunwales down to the ground and concealed both the wagon and the four horses that moved it. From a little distance one saw what appeared to be a real ship. He sent forth messengers to all of the lords of the region to announce that he would hold a tournament on the meadow below Viscount Richard's castle and that he himself would arrive by ship. Since the castle was miles from any navigable water, more than a thousand people hurried there to see what he had in mind.

"On the day appointed—a day, incidentally, when the viscount was away on business—Sir Maurice boarded his ship, sailed along the road with his crew busily plying the oars, and cast anchor at a grove below the castle. He was greeted enthusiastically by the waiting crowd. Since he was an expert at jousting, Sir Maurice further distinguished himself during the tournament that followed, and at day's end believed that he had so honored his ladylove that he had every right to expect a lover's reward. However, when he entered the lady's bedroom that night to collect it, he had a rude surprise.

"The lady had been flattered by his attentions and had enjoyed living out a love song up to this point, but, confronted by reality, she remembered that she was a married lady and ordered him to leave at once. When he refused, she called the servants, who beat him unmercifully and threw him out of the castle. So what had been a day of triumph ended with public ridicule and disgrace.

"There is a lesson for you here, my young poet," the scribe then told me. "Don't confuse fiction and real life. Within its particular framework, fiction should be plausible, but in real life anything can happen." It was good advice and later, while working on narrative poetry, I recalled it often. Don't try to copy reality, I told myself, it's illogical and has no plot.

"What was the nature of Sir Rupert's mission in France?" I asked.

"It was when the emperor held Richard the Lion-hearted captive," replied Karl. "Heinrich demanded a huge ransom so that the English king could no longer afford to support the revolt of the duke of Saxony. Richard agreed to have it paid, but his brother John and King Philip of France did not want him set free and asked the emperor to send delegates to discuss the matter. Although they offered an even greater sum to get

Richard turned over to them, the emperor, through his agents, felt bound to honor the settlement with Richard. Sir Rupert was one of the delegates."

Wildenberg was much different from Werthheim. Below the latter castle were meadows and cultivated fields, and several villages could be seen in the distance. But Wildenberg appeared entirely isolated. Closely hemmed in by the forest on three sides, the only view was to the north, looking down from the cliff. From here one could see far out over the tree-tops, which seemed to form a thick, green carpet that extended to higher ridges miles away. The forest even hid the river below, that could be traced only by the fog that usually hung over it.

Actually Wildenberg was not quite as remote from other habitations as it appeared, for only three hours away to the northwest, where the river emerged from the forest, was the town of Amorbach. It had a market, a church, and a large Benedictine monastery, the abbot of which was a friend of my great uncle. When the latter heard that I was going to Wildenberg, he asked me to deliver his greeting and good wishes to the Amorbach abbot.

The chief entertainment of Sir Rupert's retainers and guests was hunting with falcons or hounds—on foot, for the tangle of vines and fallen trees made it impossible to chase after the hounds on horseback. These hunting parties were often quite elaborate events. On the river bank a large pavilion was set up, where the ladies would sit and chat or play games while the men hunted. When the latter returned, there would be a feast, which would be followed by stringed music and singing or the recitation of short verse romances. Sometimes tents were brought down as sleeping quarters, and the hunting party would last for several days. On one occasion Emperor Heinrich and his retinue took part in the hunt and the following festivities.

The hunts took place throughout the forest except for a mountain side in the east. After I had been at Wildenberg for several months, I noticed this and asked Karl if there was any reason to avoid the area. When he seemed a little embarrassed at the question, I became curious and pressed him for an answer. "It's just an old custom that the baron chooses to observe," he said. "You know 'The Song of the Nibelungs' and will remember that it tells how Siegfried slew the dragon Fafnir and, save for one spot on his back, became invulnerable to weapons by bathing in its blood.

"Well, according to local legend, Fafnir was severely wounded and appeared to be dead, but it was only a ruse; dragons don't die easily. When Siegfried went his way, Fafnir decided to leave the country so that he would never again encounter the hero. He traveled slowly and painfully southward, by night because he was so weak that even an ordinary warrior might have slain him. While passing through the Desolate Forest, he discovered a cave that went far back into the mountain, one well suited for an injured dragon, and he crawled in to recover. In six months his wounds were healed and, frightfully hungry, he left the cave in search of a meal. To his delight the forest was filled with deer and bears that for a clever hunter were not too hard to catch.

"The Desolate Forest became Fafnir's adopted home, and he could have lived here in peace if he had moved about more carefully. But he broke down so many saplings going to and fro that there was something like a broad highway leading to his cave. Then the dragon learned that the forest had another lord, for Tarn resolved to drive him away. Time after time the sprite took him by surprise, struck him a mighty blow with a heavy club, and flowed away as a waterfall before the dragon could counterattack. But even the heaviest of clubs is less lethal than the wondrous sword that Siegfried wielded, and Fafnir was an especially stubborn dragon, who would rather put up with the bumps and bruises than leave his comfortable cave and a forest filled with game.

"Finally the sprite gathered certain herbs and prepared about fifty pounds of a powerful sleeping potion. He then killed a deer, stuffed its carcass with the potion, and placed it by night at the mouth of the cave. Fafnir woke up very hungry, as usual, and gulped down the fresh meat as soon as he saw it. Then he returned to the depth of the cave for his morning nap. He has slept there ever since. But you know how noisy hunters are, with their horns and barking hounds they would awaken Fafnir if anything could. 'Let sleeping dragons lie' is one of our favorite sayings."

"Has anyone ever gone into the cave to see if there is any basis for the legend?" I asked.

"When standing at the entrance, one can clearly hear a distant snoring sound," he replied. "Although this is not proof that the legend is factual, it has been enough to satisfy everyone's curiosity up till now."

A week or two after my arrival, I rode to Amorbach to see Abbot Erhard, as I had promised. He was a kindly old monk and was greatly pleased to hear from my uncle. He seemed very proud of the abbey, that had been his home for over forty years, and insisted on showing me around. It was indeed spacious and splendid; the abbey church with its four towers was most impressive. "The monastery was founded in the year 734 by Saint Pirmin," he told me, "and almost every abbot since his time has added something. Let me show you my addition: it's called the Felix Chapel."

The chapel was an alcove off of the nave of the church. Behind and above a low altar was a fine mural which showed a gray-haired monk looking up at a white bird that was perched on a branch just above his head. Higher up was a chorus of angels. "Would you please interpret the picture," I asked. "I have recently taken quite an interest in angels, and may put some into a Grail story I am composing."

"With pleasure," said Erhard, "for it is an important chapter in the monastery's history." This is the abbot's account:

Felix was a monk in the monastery, the most pious and the best liked of the community at that time. Humble as Job, he had no ill will toward anyone and did not scold, no matter what was done to him; he did not repay any injury in kind, but submitted to everything without anger and spent many hours a day doing true penance on his knees in prayer. Felix was deeply interested in heaven and read everything about it that he could find. It was thus revealed to him that in heaven there was joy without sorrow and without end, limitless joy so great that a thousand tongues could not tell it all.

One morning after matins while Felix was sitting on a bench just outside the gate, he read in the Holy Scriptures that "eye hath not seen, nor ear heard, neither have entered into the heart of man, the things which God hath prepared for them that love Him." Such constant bliss seemed impossible and he began to doubt it. Then God sent an angel down from heaven in the form of a little, white bird that perched on a low bough and revealed the joy of heaven in wondrous song. It sang with such charm that, closing the book, the monk sprang to his feet, so enraptured that he did not know where he was. Whatever delights he had ever known seemed nothing to him, so sweetly did the bird sing. No one who heard it could ever be distressed; the music of a thousand harps would not have been so lovely. The angelic greeting filled the monk with ecstasy.

Thinking that he might be able to catch the bird, Felix began to walk toward it, but it flew off a short distance and sang again with such enchantment that the monk nearly lost his senses: he felt as if he were in heaven. Then it flew away. "Oh if you would only come back!" cried the monk in distress. "I would give anything to hear you again. Your lovely song takes away all troubles." He could hardly bear the loss.

Just then a bell rang out, telling the mid-morning hour, and, concerned at having neglected his duties, the monk hurried back to the gate, which now was closed. "Dear brother, let me in," he called to the gate-keeper.

"Who are you?" was the reply.

"Why I am Felix," said the monk surprised. "Everybody knows me."

"I don't," declared the gate-keeper. "I never saw you in all the thirty years I've been at this monastery."

"Brother, for the sake of our dear Lord, do not make fun of me," said Felix. "I read the Scripture at the mass this morning and sang the response. I left right after matins and was delighted and bewildered by the sweet singing of a little bird."

"Go away, you are drunk," said the gate-keeper. "I'll not let you in."

But when Felix begged to see the abbot, the monk agreed to bring him and soon returned with a man whom Felix had never seen. "Abbot," said the gatekeeper, "this monk maintains that he is a member of our monastery and even that he read the Scripture here this morning." Although Felix was beginning to wonder if he were in his right mind, he gave his name and related all that had happened to him that day.

"Your story is indeed remarkable," said the strange abbot. "Come in, and we'll see what we can find out." He then led Felix to a brother who was very old. "This man insists that he has belonged to our company," he told the ancient monk. "He is called Felix. What can you tell us?"

"Long ago, when I was a novice," was the reply, "I heard about a monk named Felix. Perhaps he will be mentioned in our register."

The book was brought and, after a long search, the abbot found this entry, written exactly a century before to the day: "Felix has vanished without a trace. He was a holy man with exemplary habits who shone like a crystal before all the monks. Perhaps God has translated him."

What a wonder! The hundred years had seemed to Felix little more than an hour, but, after all this time, he had not aged, nor had his clothing rotted away. All because of the angel's singing. He was welcomed by the monks and till his death, five years later, was treated as a saint. And why not, for he had known in life the perfect joy of the saints in heaven. The records of the monastery showed that he died in 1152, the year in which Barbarossa was elected King of Germany and crowned Holy Roman Emperor.

What a country for a poet, I thought with delight; a water sprite, a dragon, and now an angel! I thanked the good abbot, promised to return sometime and sing for the brothers, and rode back to Wildenberg.

Karl's instructions were to translate the French text for me—my knowledge of French was still limited—and write down my German version. At my request, he agreed to teach me to read and write as we went along. I was to look over his shoulder and follow his finger as he read the French aloud and then translated it into German. We began by going through the entire manuscript, then we started over and took up the separate episodes one by one. During the first reading, I was truly excited by the French work and even more by the possible improvements that occurred to me. I was glad that the romance was incomplete, for it gave me the opportunity to devise an ending without being influenced at all by another poet.

Soon we established a routine. After Karl translated an episode or part of one in the morning, I worked with it during the day—altering it to suit my preference and putting it into verse—and the following morning he wrote it down and translated the next event. Now and then he offered suggestions, which were welcome, but seldom fruitful.

Step by step I accompanied my untutored and headstrong hero when he left the clearing in the forest to which his mother, Queen Herzeloyde, had retired and stopped in turn at the pavilion of Duke Orilus, the court of King Arthur at Nantes, the castle of Gurnemanz, the city of Belrepeire, the Grail Castle of Munsalvæsche, and the pavilions of Arthur's court along the bank of the Plimizoel River. I looked on with pleasure when he broke the siege of Belrepeire and married its beautiful Queen Condwiramurs and when he defeated the boastful Keye; I grieved when he caused the death of his mother, brought much suffering on the lovely Jeschute, killed the gallant King Ither, and failed to relieve the suffering of his uncle, the Grail king; I sympathized fully with his sad longing at the Plimizoel, for I too sorely missed my dear wife; I felt his humiliation when he was denounced and vilified before all the knights of the Round Table; and, yes, I shared his wrath at God for permitting him to err tragically at Munsalvæsche when he was only following a wise man's teaching. But I did not interfere; in fiction as in life, a man must act in accordance with his nature whatever the cost. Parzival must now set out on a long search for the Grail and years of jousting to prove that no knight had as great a right to find it as he.

When I came to Wildenberg I expected to complete my task before spring, but by the time my hero reached this point it was already April and the book was only about one-fourth of its eventual size: nearly 25,000 verses. Still the romance had reached a point where it could stand by itself, so my host had something that could be read to his guests. I therefore asked leave to return to Eschenbach. I knew I was needed there and, besides that, I was homesick. The baron paid me quite well for my labor when we parted. "I'll listen to what you have done," he said, "and send word if I want you to come back in the fall and continue the work."

On the second evening of the journey to Eschenbach, I pitched my tent in a grassy clearing by the river just outside of Würzburg. While I was preparing a meal, another knight—

accompanied by a squire and a page—stopped and set up camp nearby. He introduced himself as Wirnt of Grafenberg, north of Erlangen, and said that he was returning from visiting kinsmen in Frankfurt. I was pleased when he added that he knew some of my songs. "Have you composed any narrative poetry?" he asked.

"Yes," I replied, "for the past six months I have been preparing a German version of a French Arthurian romance."

"What a coincidence!" he exclaimed. "While I was in Frankfurt, a squire told me a French story about one of King Arthur's knights, and I have decided to retell it, or something quite similar, in German verse. At fifty-two, I am a little old to become a poet, but my eldest son has taken charge of my estates, and I shall have plenty of time to work at it."

"You must tell me the story when we have eaten," I said. "I promise never to use it in any way."

"Gladly," he replied. So after we had finished our meal and a bottle of some excellent wine that Sir Wirnt had brought with him, he related an unusual tale, a summary of which is as follows:

During the festivities connected with the coronation of King Arthur a strikingly handsome and splendidly accoutered young knight appeared and asked Arthur to grant him the next quest that the king should assign. Arthur agreed and inquired about the youth's name and homeland.

"I can only tell you," was the reply, "that I come from a land which is almost surrounded by the sea and is ruled by my mother's brother. I don't know my father's name; he left before I was born and is never mentioned. As for my own name, I have been called: 'dear son,' 'dear boy,' and 'young lord;' nothing else."

"How odd!" exclaimed Arthur. "We shall call you 'The Handsome Stranger' and you shall stay at my court until there is need for a knight's service." The following morning a richly dressed young lady, accompanied by a dwarf, appeared and introduced herself as the messenger of a princess, who implored the king to send the boldest of his knights—one ready to face the greatest danger—to rescue her.

"This is my quest!" cried The Handsome Stranger.

"It's no task for a mere youth," declared the messenger.

"Perhaps you should wait for another undertaking," the king suggested to the knight.

"No, my lord," said the latter. "I have your promise."

"And I shall keep it," answered Arthur. "May good fortune attend you."

The journey to the princess's castle was interrupted by frequent combats. The first was at a ford which was guarded by a fierce knight, whom The Handsome Stranger defeated; the second was with two evil giants, whom he slew; five more victories followed, all against individual knights. One evening the three reached a bridge that led to a city and a splendid castle that was separated from the mainland by an arm of the sea. When they started to cross over to find lodging for the night, The Handsome Stranger was attacked by the knight who guarded the bridge, a man whose custom it was to cut off the heads of those he defeated and place them on the gate. After an especially long and bitter struggle, the bridge guard was killed; thereupon the travelers were welcomed by the townspeople.

The castle's mistress was beautiful beyond description. Leading him to her quarters, she offered the youth her heart and hand if he would remain with her. He was strongly tempted to do so, but, when he returned to his companions, the messenger reminded him of his promise to aid the princess. Therefore the three stole away before daybreak to continue their journey. Two days later they arrived at their goal, a splendid but completely deserted city, and rode into a large and mysterious palace. Here The Handsome Stranger was attacked by a powerful rider whose steed had a horn on its forehead and breathed flames. When the exhausted youth finally managed to kill his antagonist, the castle was enveloped in complete darkness.

This was soon broken by the fiery breath of a huge dragon that slowly approached the travelers. Its head was enormous, black, and shaggy; its beak was bare, a fathom long and a yard wide, pointed in front and sharp as a newly whetted spear; in its jaws were teeth like the tusks of a boar. Broad, horny scales covered it, and a sharp spine—like that with which a crocodile cuts ships in two—went from head to tail. For the first time in his life The Handsome Stranger was afraid, but he drew his sword and stood his ground. "Don't strike it under any condition!" commanded the messenger, "and don't move. I'll tell you what to do." The monster came nearer and stretched its great, dreadful head out to the knight, who obeyed his companion although he expected to be swallowed down in a single gulp. "Kiss it!" she ordered.

"What?" he cried astonished.

"Kiss the dragon!" she demanded.

"Well, why not?" thought The Handsome Stranger. "If I were not weary and had a sturdy spear and were mounted on a fresh charger, I might have a chance against this beast. But, tired as I am, a struggle with only a sword would be futile." So he leaned forward, kissed the horny beak, and fainted.

When the youth opened his eyes, he stared into those of a lovely maiden who had bent over him and was rubbing his face with a cool, wet cloth. "Who are you?" he gasped.

"I am the princess whom you have saved," she replied. "The man whom you have just killed is a magician. He placed my city under a spell, gave me the form, but not the strength of a dragon, and said I would remain thus until I agreed to marry him or until a knight was bold enough to kiss me without knowing my true identity. You have done so and in gratitude I offer you my hand and my kingdom."

The Handsome Stranger assured the lady that he was glad to have served her, but did not at once respond to her offer. He had intended to return to the beautiful mistress of the island as soon as his mission was completed, yet, as he now pondered the matter, something bothered him: the heads on the gate. What kind of woman would let her gatekeeper collect such mementos from innocent travelers? Would his own head be really safe? "Dear princess," he said, "I would be greatly pleased and honored to be your husband."

The wedding was attended by King Arthur and all the knights of the Round Table. It was then that the Handsome Stranger learned that his name was Guinglain and that the renowned Sir Gawain was his father.

"It is a fine story," I told Sir Wirnt, "and I trust that your version will be even better."

"I'll make some changes," he said. "I think that I'll begin with Sir Gawain and relate in detail how he happened to come to the land by the sea and why he left." In the morning we said goodbye and went our separate ways. I never saw Sir Wirnt again, but I have heard his Arthurian romance read. It is an excellent work, much better indeed than his source.

It was delightful to be home again with my family after a six-month absence. And the landscape here, with its pastures, plowed fields, and peaceful village, was somewhat more to my liking than the great, dense forest that, save for the one castle—which it appeared to resent—showed no signs of human habitation. Brother Andrew came down from Ansbach to help with our May Day celebration, and we played and sang for the dancing villagers all afternoon. I selected a variety of songs from many different poet-composers—not including myself—to see which one the peasants liked best. They chose this song by Walther of Vogelweide:

> Under the linden
> I and my lover
> softly were bedded in grass and shade.
> And if you should wander
> there, you'll discover
> many a broken bloom and blade.
> By the forest, in the dale,
> 'tandaradei!'
> sweetly sang the nightingale.

I went to our meeting
and did not tarry,
for he I loved had gone before.
Oh, what a greeting!
Holy Mary,
I'll be blessed for evermore!
Did he kiss me? Yes, and how!
'Tandaradei.'
See how red my lips are now.

My lover had laid
with care meanwhile
a lovely bed of flowers for me.
The village maid
will slyly smile
who walks there past the linden tree
and sees the spot where on that day
'tandaradei'
my head among the roses lay.

If anyone guesses
that we were together
(may God forbid!), I'd surely die.
Of his caresses,
hid by the heather,
may no one know but he and I
and the bird that sang so well:
'tandaradei.'
I can trust it not to tell.

One reason they preferred this song, I suppose, is that it does not treat a lady and her knight, but a peasant girl and her lover. I'm fond of it too.

"Why don't we let the monks hear the same songs," said Brother Andrew, "and see which one they like best. I am sure that the abbot would be delighted to have us perform at the monastery."

I agreed to do so, and the following week rode to Ansbach. One of the brothers, a tall, portly man named Wilhelm, had a fine tenor voice, and I persuaded him to sing the woman's stanzas in those songs that consisted of dialogue. He proved to have considerable talent as an actor and played his role to the amused delight of the audience. The monks' favorite was this dawn song by Heinrich of Morungen, a serious fellow who might not have approved of the spirit in which it was performed:

Knight:

"Oh! Oh!
Will nevermore the glow
of that fair form as white
as newly fallen snow
come to me through the night?
I thought I saw arise
the bright moon in the skies.
Then came the dawn."

Lady:

"Oh! Oh!
And will he never know
the daybreak here again,
nor watch the darkness go,
nor share my sorrow when
I cry: 'Alas, it's day!'?
That he, too, used to say
when he beside me lay.
Then came the dawn!"

Knight:

"Oh! Oh!
A thousand times, it seems
she kissed me as I slept,
and till I left my dreams,
how bitterly she wept.
But then I knew how best
to put her tears to rest;
she drew me to her breast.
Then came the dawn!"

Lady:

"Oh! Oh!
So many times has he
seen more than was his due
and quite uncovered me;
he wanted just to view
poor me, all bare and bright.
I wondered that my knight
so much enjoyed the sight.
Then came the dawn!"

The summer passed pleasantly and too quickly. The courtiers

at Wertheim and Wildenberg thought that living at Eschenbach with only peasants to talk to must be dreadfully boring, but I found peasants and their manners quite interesting. The chief reason I composed songs and romances about lords and ladies is that they could afford to pay me for my labors. My knowledge of what went on in the village came largely from the meier and my wife's maids; the former told what I needed to know, the latter kept us abreast of the gossip, including a recent unforgettable experience of the peasant Willibrand.

Willibrand had married Kriemhild, who was the prettiest maiden for miles around. This was perhaps unfortunate, for he was very jealous and constantly feared that someone might persuade her to be unfaithful. He really had no reason to distrust his wife, but could not be convinced that she would never yield to the entreaties of another. Moreover, in addition to working his plot of land, he was a teamster and, as such, was frequently away over night, which added to his concern. The uncertainty about his wife's fidelity troubled him so much that he finally asked his brother Adelbert, a single and handsome young man, to find out if she could be seduced.

Adelbert was persistent and could not be discouraged. Every morning as Kriemhild drove her cows to the meadow he appeared, assured her of his undying love, and suggested a secret meeting. When she came to get the cattle in the evening, he was there again. She became more and more upset by his ceaseless wooing and one day, while she was washing clothes at the river bank with three of her friends, she broke down and wept bitterly. "What's the matter?" cried her companions astonished, and she told them about her importunate suitor.

"What can I do?" she wailed. "My husband is very fond of Adelbert and would not believe me if I told of his proposals. He would say that I was just trying to make trouble between them."

"I have a plan," said tall Greta. "Tell Adelbert to come to your house at night when your husband is gone. Say that you will put a single candle in the kitchen window to show that you are alone. And leave the rest to Irmgart and Bertha here and me."

The following morning Kriemhild told her suitor that Willibrand would be gone and the back door would be unlatched when a candle was burning in the window. Adelbert was quite pleased to see that no woman was so virtuous that she could resist his charm and guile. But his brother was not at all pleased at the report about his wife. "Tomorrow I'll yoke my oxen and pretend to set out for Nuremberg," he said, "but after dark I'll return and come to see her in your place. I'll teach the hussy a lesson she'll never forget."

True to his word, Willibrand slipped into the dark house that night, but, before he could light a lamp, tall Greta seized him by the hair from behind and threw him to the floor. Then she, Irmgart, and Bertha beat him with sturdy rods. Despite his pleas and cries of pain, they thrashed him until he was bruised from head to toe. At last, they dragged the supposed suitor to the door and threw him out.

Willibrand crept back to where he had left his wagon, drove to the nearby woods, and hid there until noon of the following day. Then he returned home and explained the bruises on his face by saying that he had fallen. Although his flesh and bones were sore for at least six months, he was happy to be reassured of Kriemhild's constancy and was never again tempted to test her.

I don't know how the whole affair, as I heard it, came to light, but somehow such things do. I have often told the story to young bridegrooms with this warning: better betrayed than beaten.

Since the crops that year were bountiful, our October harvest festival was especially joyous. As usual, mass was followed by a colorful procession to a shrine about two miles away, then by a great feast. Tables were set up in the meadow beside the river, and all the villagers sat down together to eat and drink their fill under the clear Autumn sky. Afterwards there were sports and dancing for those still able to take part. Most of the songs I sang for the dancers were the glutton and drinking songs that were now being composed, but not by me. It was such a happy time and place that I was somewhat disappointed the next day when a messenger came from Baron Rupert, asking me to return to Wildenberg and continue my romance. I would not have done it for the gold alone, but I had become so captivated by this young Parzival that I could not leave him.

A week later I set out for Wildenberg on my charger and leading a packhorse. As always on a long trip, I wore mail beneath my cloak and a sword at my side; a helmet hung from my neck. "A man is his own best guardian," father liked to say. Just beyond Ansbach I overtook two merchants—mounted on mules and leading four heavily laden donkeys—who had come from Ingolstadt and were traveling to Würzburg with their wares. Seeing that I was armed, they asked if I would ride with them, for they had heard that there were robbers along the way who preyed especially on merchants. They offered to pay for my protection.

Although they traveled more slowly than I, we reached an agreement and rode on together. We were going through the hills north of Uffenheim when four riders dashed from the edge of the forest. They apparently had not expected to encounter a knight in armor, for they hesitated on seeing one, then came on—two straight at me, two at the train of pack animals. Their purpose was obvious: they intended to keep me occupied while leading the donkeys away. They had not learned that two men in wool coats are hardly a match for one warrior encased in steel.

I rode at the two, turned to the outside, where only one of the robbers could reach me, then slammed my powerful steed into the flank of his horse, causing it to stumble. Before the rider regained his balance, I took off his head and, swinging around, charged at the second robber. After a few exchanges of blows, he fell and I hurried to the aid of the merchants. They were doing quite well. They had leaped from their mules—that are not good battle steeds—and were defending the donkeys with iron bars that had been concealed under their saddle blankets. When their opponents saw me coming, they fled.

The conflict, if one could call it that, was a trivial matter, and I mention it only as an observer of social change. The robber class had deteriorated greatly in the preceding decades. It had once consisted of impoverished noblemen who knew something of combat, but by then it was made up largely of run-away peasants on stolen palfreys. The merchant class, on the other hand, had become more confident and aggressive in protecting its wares. I collected the spoils of battle from the dead men—two palfreys and two plain, but serviceable swords—and we went on to Würzburg, where the merchants sold them for me. Two days later I rode up the mountain side to Wildenberg.

Since I had been thinking about it all summer, the romance moved forward at a rapid pace. My hero had gotten a little hard to understand. A dauntless and peerless warrior who stubbornly aspired to the highest honor known to mankind, he was also loyal, sensitive, and capable of undying love and deep sorrow. I finally decided to add a sort of introduction and tell of his father Gahmuret, who was the light-hearted descendant of a fairy and the greatest of all soldiers of fortune. Between them, he and Parzival's faithful, self-denying mother reveal the diverse hereditary sources of Parzival's chief traits, that often caused him to be at war with himself.

An account of Gahmuret also enabled me to begin the romance with descriptions of knighthood on a grand scale, as he paraded his splendid entourage into Moorish Patelmunt to the music of flutes, fiddles, drums, and trumpets; then lifted the siege of the city with his strength and martial skills, married its queen, and became the lord of the Kingdom of Zazamanc. When he tired of inactivity and fled to Spain, I was able to portray at length the most colorful of tournaments—one in which all the famous lords of his time took part—and show Gahmuret winning, with amusing reluctance, the hand of a second queen, Parzival's mother. I hoped that an impressive display of chivalry would so arouse the listener's interest that it would not flag through the thousands of verses that chronicled the less spectacular, but more significant, events that followed.

So much for Gahmuret, but why did the Arthurian knight Gawain take up such a large portion of a romance about the education of Parzival to become the Grail king? I have often been asked that question. If it was a mistake, it was not mine. Gawain entered the story at an opportune time—when Parzival was about to depart on his angry, four-year campaign to prove himself worthy of finding the Grail. What should I do? Just go back to Eschenbach and wait for his return? Of course not. Since Gawain was starting out on his own eventful travels, I decided to go along and tell about them until Parzival came back. Moreover, the story needed some adventures that were a little humorous to balance those of Parzival that were mostly rather tragic.

Gawain was the true knight of courtly love song, although a rather amusing one. I thought the first lady-love of his journey was the most charming. It was a child's game when little Obilot, Duke Lyppaut's seven-year-old daughter, chose him as her knight, but the successful completion of the task she assigned him brought an end to the strife and enmity between her father and King Meljanz. I could have laughed heartily at Gawain's encounter with the second lady, the beautiful Antikonie, whose lusty desire matched his own, if I had not feared that it would cost him his life. When he escaped death, I left him for a time, because Parzival had unexpectedly returned.

The ensuing episode, in which my hero confessed to his hermit uncle his sin of blaming personal misfortunes on God and then learned about the Grail and the Grail Kingdom, brought me considerable undeserved criticism. When I described the Grail as a wondrous stone brought down from heaven by the neutral angels—those who did not take sides in the conflict between God and Lucifer—and told how it supplied the Grail knights and maidens with everything they needed, I only repeated the account of my source, the French Kyot. On being advised that later French narratives called the chalice of the Last Supper the Grail, I replied that the Grail of Sir Heinrich of Türlin's romance resembled a reliquary, so it was possible for several holy objects to have the same name. And when clerics accused me of being anti-Church for having Parzival's sin declared forgiven by a layman instead of a priest, I reminded them that at the same time I spoke highly of priests.

The most bitter objection came from a bishop who heard the manuscript read before it was completed and attacked me for saying that I did not know whether or not God forgave the neutral angels. Since Sir Rupert was a little concerned at this, I agreed to alter the statement, but, instead of discarding the sheet of good vellum on which it was written, I confessed later in the work that I had made a mistake, that God had surely damned those angels. But now I return to my original statement. How would I know what God did?

Exactly 8400 verses were composed that winter and, although I found the activities of Parzival and Gawain most interesting, by April I was tired of recording them and eager to go home. I promised to return to Wildenberg in the fall, took leave of Sir Rupert, and set out for Eschenbach. The afternoon of the fourth day of the journey was unseasonably warm and, when I came abreast of an isolated farm outside the village of Ermetzhofen, I turned off the road to get a drink for myself and my two horses. The owner, who was sitting in the shade of a tree in front of the house, was most cordial. On hearing my request, he urged me to dismount and sit down on his bench while he cared for my needs. Going to the well, he drew several buckets of water and emptied them in a trough for my steed and packhorse, then brought a full pitcher to me. In the meantime a painting on the gable of the house caught my attention. It portrayed a huge white beast with a long neck that I assumed was a polar bear, although I had never seen one. When I asked about it, the peasant related an unusual experience of his grandfather, a well-to-do peasant named Ortwin.

One of the first acts of Barbarossa as emperor was to end the succession struggle in Denmark by declaring Erich Emunds' son Svend to be the rightful king. In gratitude the latter dispatched an attendant to Swabia with a tame polar bear as a gift for his benefactor. Since the journey took five or six weeks, the man, on horseback, leading the bear, on foot, had to make many stops along the way. One was at Ortwin's farm. Seeing the peasant sitting on a bench before the house, the Dane rode up and asked if he could purchase a meal and a night's lodging for himself and his two animals.

"First tell me, friend," said Ortwin. "What is that fearful beast? Is it a natural creature or a monster?"

"It's just a bear," the Dane assured him, "and quite tame. It comes from Norway, a land of ice and snow, and my lord, the king of Denmark, is sending it to the emperor."

"Well, I'll gladly feed you," said the peasant, "but lodging you is another matter. Some devil or monster takes over my dwelling at night. I haven't seen it, but it is very strong and it drives people and cattle out with mighty blows. My family and I sleep in a shed by the field, the cattle remain on the meadow. Everything in the house and barn is topsy-turvy. The terrible creature throws tables, chairs, chests, pots, and pans here and there as it rages about. So, as you see, I am unable to offer you shelter."

"My steed will be all right on the meadow," replied the Dane, "but I would like to be protected from the damp and cold, and the bear must stay with me. Be so kind as to let me go inside. Perhaps God will shield me from this devil."

"You're welcome to enter," replied Ortwin, "but you will surely regret it." Then the good peasant brought plenty of beer, bread, and ham for his guest and a side of lamb for the bear. Crossing himself, the pious Dane led the bear into the house, then into the kitchen, where he made a fire to broil the ham. Both man and beast were hungry and tired from the day's journey. When they had eaten their fill, the bear lay down by the fire, but the man, with the caution for which Danes are noted, climbed into the oven and closed the oven door except for a narrow crack.

He was almost asleep when he heard a noise and, peering through the crack, saw a horrible looking kobold—hardly three spans tall—rush into the kitchen and spring toward the fire. The creature wore a red cape and carried an iron spit on which was impaled a piece of meat. He sat down and began to broil the meat for his supper. When he saw the sleeping bear, he started up but did nothing at first. Yet the longer he stared at it the more angry he became; that was clear to the Dane. Finally the kobold made up his mind and gave the bear a blow on the neck with the spit. It curled back its lips, snarled, and went back to sleep.

The spiteful, ill-tempered kobold continued to broil the meat until he saw that it was really sizzling; then he raised the spit high over his head and struck the tired bear across the muzzle with all his strength. Now fully aroused, the bear sprang up and rushed so swiftly at the kobold that he could not escape. It seized him with its paws and began fiercely to bite and claw, causing him to cry out in pain. But, although small, he was powerful and could bite, scratch, and gouge with such effect that the great bear roared with rage and fury. Its wild cry resounded all through the house and the courtyard. Bear and kobold struggled in mortal combat: first the kobold, then the bear was on top as they fought back and forth. The Dane was sad at heart to see how rudely his bear was treated. The combat continued until almost midnight, when the kobold was at last defeated. He screamed and fled, and the bear, worn out from the conflict, lay down again and rested his battle-weary limbs.

At daybreak the Dane crawled out of the oven and led his charge from the house. The peasant, who had heard the uproar, stood at the gate and greeted him warmly. "I'm glad to see that you are still alive, my good man," he said. Recounting the events in a few words, the Dane fetched his steed and journeyed on, leading the tattered bear.

When Ortwin got his oxen from the meadow and began to plow his field, the kobold ran up and sprang onto a rock above the peasant. His legs were covered with blood, his little body was scratched and bitten, his tiny cape was ripped and torn. "Listen you! Listen you! Listen you!" he called out fiercely to the plowman. "Is your big cat still alive?"

"Yes it is," replied Ortwin, "and last night it bore me five splendid kittens, white and long-bodied, all just like their mother. You must go look at them. You never saw such pretty cats."

"Why should I look at them!" cried the kobold. "I've been hurt. Just the one nearly killed me. Six would eat me alive. I'll never come back to your farm again." The creature disappeared, and Ortwin returned to his house, moved in, and afterwards dwelt there in peace. To make sure that the kobold did not forget the bear, he had a likeness of it painted for all to see.

I thanked the peasant for the water and the bit of family history and went on my way. Two days later I was at home, listening to mother tell the story of the prince and the fairy queen to her two granddaughters and grandson while my wife and a maid sewed bright summer dresses for the Whitsuntide and May Day festivals. The children were larger, otherwise, thank God, nothing had changed. The following day I talked with the meier, who wanted me to get Count Poppo's permission to clear some of the untended forest to the east so that the villagers would have more meadow land. I promised, although somewhat regretfully, to present their request. I knew that the peasants needed more land, but I regretted the loss of primeval forest.

A week later our family rode the river trail to see our kinfolk in Abenberg—all except mother, who was now too frail for the difficult trip. "Some day," I thought, "much of this forest will be gone and the rest will be cleared. All of the mystery and romance will vanish; there will be no home for wood nymphs, water sprites, and the like—real or imaginary—and children will laugh scornfully at tales of them. The three ravines and two fords will be bridged, and what is now adventure will be a short, uneventful outing."

This spring I noticed for the first time that, while Eschenbach and its ways were much the same as they had been since I was a child, the world outside was changing. The towns and cities were growing, there was much more traffic on the roads, and there were empty houses in some old villages. "It's trade," I thought. "There is too much trade." Moreover, it seemed to me that there was a decline in both courtly and village manners. "Wolfram," I told myself, "at thirty-six you are already showing signs of old age." Hardly two decades later, I saw many of my forebodings realized. Forests were retreating to the mountains, villagers went to the towns to buy goods that they once made themselves, and poetry was didactic and dull. I was glad that I had decided that the latter part of my Parzival romance should have plenty of secular magic to go with its Grail miracles.

I visited Abbot Hugo several times during the summer, sang for the monks twice, and once told them the story of Parzival as far as I had gotten with it. My memory at that time was so good that I could recite much of it by heart. I was encouraged by the enthusiastic response, for I had sometimes wondered if my verses were doing justice to the subject. After the applause had subsided, the abbot said: "Now Brother Wilhelm will sing a song for you. You are not familiar with it, for both the verses and the music were recently composed by our Brother Andrew. I consider it one of the best of the many in praise of the Virgin Mary and I hope it will become well known." I liked both the words and the melody and often sang it at church festivals. This is how it goes:

Ave Maria, rose without a thorn,
with evil deeds that I must mourn
have I betrayed Him thou hast born.
Maria, save me from His scorn.

Ave Maria, because thy Child is dead
Who hung before thee and was red
with blood, help me receive the bread
of angels, when in death and dread.

Ave Maria, because His life blood stole
from Him and racked with pain thy soul,
just as the angry billows roll,
help me to reach a joyful goal.

Ave Maria, thou so true and kind,
O let an angel be assigned
to me when I leave the world behind.
Keep me from what the foe designed.

The abbot was at that time quite optimistic about the political situation in Germany. "Pope Innocence has finally recognized Philip as our rightful monarch," he told me. "It will now be easy for the king to force Otto and his supporters to do the same. But I don't trust that Italian pope. He regards all the crowned heads of Europe as his subjects and claims the right to appoint all of Germany's bishops. If he had his way, even the monasteries would be governed by him. Still, the condition of the country has improved."

It was raining in late October when I started out for Wildenberg, and there was constant drizzle all the way to Wertheim. The count and countess gave me a warm welcome and asked me to stay for several days, which I was glad to do, because all my clothes were soaking wet and my two horse were nearly exhausted from the long marches along muddy roads. The castle was filled with guests, who were being entertained with dancing, singing, games, and story telling. I contributed to the festivities with renditions of love songs and with an account of my romance, as far as it had progressed. I was delighted with the reception it received.

Most of the diversion was supplied by a minstrel from Strassburg whose repertoire included both French and German songs and dances. Also, on two successive evenings, he gave an account of the travels of Alexander of Macedonia in the Far East. The part that interested me most appeared in a letter that Alexander is supposed to have sent to Aristotle, and, since it perhaps has been completely forgotten, I'll retell his adventure.

"Once, while we were travelling along the seashore," wrote the great emperor, "I rode away from the army with three thousand men to look for anything marvelous. In the distance we saw a stately forest and found, when we reached it, much that was wonderful. We heard lyres and harps therein and many lovely voices singing the sweetest song ever composed by men, one that far surpassed all other music combined. It was delightful in the shade of the trees, for the ground was covered with grass, flowers, and manifold fragrant herbs. I don't believe any other forest ever contained so much beauty. This large woodland bordered on a splendid meadow where we saw many fine springs that came running, clear and cold, out of the forest. I and my brave warriors discovered marvels there that pleased us greatly; I shall tell you all about them and leave nothing out.

"We were all much impressed with the wondrous beauty of the forest. The trees were tall with such dense, widely spreading branches that no rays of the sun could reach the ground below, which was truly quite unusual. Drawn by the delightful singing, I and my men at once left our horses and entered the forest. We hurried in the direction of the music, impatient to learn what mystery it held. We found a host of lovely maidens playing on the green clover; a hundred thousand and more were dancing about and singing so beautifully that the sweet sound ringing through the forest caused me and my brave warriors, the highborn and the lowly, to forget our sorrows, our hardships, our sicknesses, and all other misfortunes that had ever befallen us. It is not surprising that all of us then felt as if we would know only joy and splendor as long as we lived. I and my men forgot every pain and care as well as whatever grief we had had from childhood on. Indeed it seemed to me that I would never again suffer any ailment or fear danger or death if I remained here.

"If you want to learn about the maidens—from whence they came and what happened to them—you may well find the story astonishing. After winter was over and everything became green with the arrival of summer, elegant flowers began to spring up in the forest. They were beautiful and gleamed brightly: their red and white could be seen from afar. No flower could be more lovely. They were round as a ball—so it seemed to us—very large, and the petals were tightly closed. When they opened up— just think—full-grown maidens stepped out.

"I am telling you just what I have heard. They were alive and thought like humans, they chatted and coaxed as maidens of about twelve do, and they were truly beautiful. I have never seen such lovely eyes and faces, and their arms, legs, and feet were as white as ermine. There was not one who was not well-mannered and charming. Light-hearted and joyful, they laughed and sang; such sweet voices have never been heard before. If you can believe it, these maidens always had to be in the shade; otherwise they could not survive, for those on whom the sun shone perished.

"It was indeed wonderful there. The forest resounded early and late with the melodious voices of birds and maidens; it was enchanting. The maidens' clothing had grown to their skin and the ribbons to their hair, and all they wore was red and snow-white like the flowers. When we saw them approaching, our hearts sprang to meet them; such delightful women are unknown to the world outside. I sent for my army at once. As soon as it arrived and the warriors heard the splendid voices, they wisely pitched their tents in the forest rather than on the meadow. We made camp with cries of joy, for we all were very pleased with our rare brides and intended to remain there. We made them our wives and were happier than ever before in our lives. Oh why did it have to end so soon!

"You can believe these marvelous events, for I observed them with my own eyes. Our life continued thus for the three months and twelve days that I and my warriors were in the green forest beside the fair meadow with the lovely women, living blissfully and sharing our joys with them. Then a great misfortune overtook us, one that I shall never cease to lament. At the end of that time our happiness came to an end, for the flowers withered and the beautiful women died. The trees lost their leaves, the springs ceased to flow, the birds stopped singing, and my heart was oppressed by grief and pain. I was terribly distressed as I watched the women die day after day. How great was my pity as I saw them perish with the flowers! Then I and my men sadly departed."

The reason why I remember this story so well is that it seemed a parable of those times. When the cold, clear light of thirteenth century reason blighted the green leaves of romance and shone down on the wondrous fantasies of an earlier age, they soon sickened and died. And what was once life and beauty became fading memories.

After three pleasant days, I went on to Wildenberg and began work at once, for I was eager to know how Gawain would fare with his third ladylove, the beautiful Duchess Orgeluse of Logroys, who wanted to use him to get vengeance on King Gramoflanz. But first he had to survive the fearful devices in the magician's Castle of Marvels: the bed that bore the knight about at breakneck speed, crashing into one wall after another; the five hundred slings that pelted him with stones as he cowered on the bed beneath his shield; and the bombardment by five hundred crossbows that followed. Then came the mighty lion that was as tall as a horse, and, after it was slain, the sorely wounded Gawain had to fight the mighty knight Turkoyt. There was enough peril and conflict in this adventure to satisfy the most bloodthirsty audience. It satisfied the scornful duchess, who finally accepted the knight as her lover, even before he was to avenge the death of her husband.

Karl said that it was a little far-fetched that Gawain's long-missing mother, grandmother, and two sisters should happen to be with the four hundred maidens whom Gawain freed at the castle. But I maintained that this was not only logical but inevitable, for the strange Grail messenger who denounced Wolfram four and a half years earlier had said that the four would be there. Should I have shown her to be a liar? Moreover, everyone knew that these members of Gawain's family had been abducted, and they had to be somewhere. Why not at the magician's castle?

The same critic thought it unlikely that King Gramoflanz's ladylove should be the sister of Gawain, whom he had sworn to kill; and that Gawain should fight Parzival, believing him to be Gramoflanz; and that this king should fight Parzival, thinking him Gawain. But I held the cases of mistaken identity to be absolutely essential, for, had Gawain and Gramoflanz fought, one would have been killed and there could have been no wedding of the king and Gawain's sister. Necessity needs not be defended as coincidence.

Well, King Arthur and his knights appeared in time to witness the marriages of Gawain, his mother, and his sisters, but what of Parzival and his quest? Since he had been denounced and humiliated by the Grail messenger before the court of King Arthur, it seemed only just that the same messenger should appear before the same court to ask Parzival's pardon and announce that he was to be lord of the Grail. If I contributed anything to the story, it was to add a little order to the natural confusion of life.

Now all that was required was for Parzival to ride to the Grail Castle, ask the compassionate question that ended his uncle's suffering, and be reunited with the beloved wife whom he had not seen in five years. Would that all earnest quests ended so happily! Of course this need not have been the end of the story, for I hinted rather broadly that I might have been willing to tell in detail the adventures of Parzival's son Lohengrin, but no sponsor rose to the bait.

It was in June of 1207 that I finished my romance and took leave of the baron and the baroness. As I rode away I felt both relieved at having finally finished a work that had occupied my mind almost constantly for nearly three years and apprehensive that I might find little of importance to replace it. My farewell to the dark, mysterious, threatening forest was almost tearful. Around it water sprite and nobleman had built an invisible wall like that which protected the park below Brandigan Castle in Hartmann of Aue's romance. May the forest be spared the changes beyond its borders! May every tree and stone be safe from human hand till Judgment Day!

Since I did not know when I might be coming north again, I decided to add three days to my journey and return by way of Bamberg and Nuremberg, cities of which I had heard much but had never seen. The road between Würzburg and Bamberg was mountainous, and I and my horses were weary when we descended to the valley of the Regnitz and entered the city. Fortunately I had been foresighted enough the preceding fall to get a letter of recommendation from Uncle Hugo, and this obtained food and comfortable quarters for the three of us at the Benedictine monastery there. The following morning one of the monks volunteered to show me about.

There was much to see: the castle, the ruins of the cathedral, the market, but what interested me most was a carving on the portal of the Church of St. James. There were three figures. At the side was an emperor of the holy Roman Empire, as was shown by the large stone at the back of his crown. He was watching a sword fight between the other two; one was a Crusader (there was a cross on his shield), the other looked like a man except for his neck and head, which resembled those of a crane.

"I suppose there is a good story behind this scene," I said to my guide."

"Indeed there is," he replied, "and the setting of the final chapter is Bamberg. It is one of our favorite legends."

"May I hear it?" I asked. "I am much interested in legends."

"The story is quite long and includes many adventures," said the monk, "but I can tell you a little about the one depicted here and give the background of the whole." We sat down on the steps leading up to the portal, and he began:

There was once a bold young duke of Bavaria named Ernst.

He was the stepson and loyal supporter of Otto the Great. But a treacherous count convinced the emperor that Ernst was conspiring against him and hoped to drive him from the throne. The quick-tempered Otto thereupon gathered an army and invaded Bavaria, the duke defended his land, and the ensuing war lasted for several years. When he could see that he could no longer withstand the forces of the Empire, Ernst announced a Crusade and set out with a large number of his knights for Constantinople. When they were sailing from there for the Holy Land, a great storm seized their ship, drove it about wildly for weeks, and finally left it just outside the harbor of an unknown land.

Not far off they saw a splendid city surrounded by a high wall of precious marble—yellow, green, blue, black, red, and white—that gleamed more brightly than glass. The stones were carefully laid out in an orderly design like a chessboard and here and there formed all sorts of pictures. Around the wall was a moat through which ran a river that completely enclosed the city. The battlements were skillfully adorned inside and out with gold and jewels, large and small, all wrought with great craft. The city did not need to fear any army, for it was strongly fortified with many-colored and artfully carved barbicans, towers, and parapets.

The Crusaders sailed into the harbor, dropped anchor, and disembarked in the small boat. "I want to find out where we are," said Ernst, "and, if possible, get more provisions. Five of you will go with me to the city, the rest will remain behind, for we do not want the natives to consider us invaders. I and those with me will be armed and in armor so that we can fight our way back if we are attacked. In this event, I'll sound my horn and you here will come to our aid. In the meantime fill our casks with water from the brook over there." When the duke and his companions reached the city, they were surprised to see the gate open and no one on either the outer or inner battlements. Crossing the bridge, they entered the city and still encountered nobody.

In a beautiful park in the middle of the city they found many chairs and tables arranged in a circle. The chairs were elegant, and the tables were covered with silk and gold cloth trimmed with finely embroidered borders. No emperor ever had as splendid a place to eat. On each table was bread, fish, the meat of tame and wild beasts, and wine from mulberry, honey, herbs, and grapes—the best to be found anywhere. Walking further, they saw stately palaces—grand and strangely formed—with arches and lofty doors that were more ornate than any others on earth and sparkled like stars. The great halls were splendid and artfully planned. Beside the most impressive of the palaces they found two streams flowing side by side, one with warm, the other with cold water. Nearby stood a fine bathhouse that was covered over with an arched roof of green marble strongly supported by buttresses. Inside gleamed red gold vats into which water flowed through two silver pipes to supply either warm or cold water.

The place was so inviting that the six might have taken a bath if they had not suddenly heard a strange cry, mighty and terrible, that came from the plain outside the walls and sounded like the screeching of a huge flock of cranes. The din was loud and frightening, as fierce a clamor as has ever been heard. Ernst led his men into the palace and up a stairway to an alcove with a window that was high above the park. Here they could look over the whole city and watch what happened inside and outside the walls without anyone seeing them. They caught sight of a strange throng of men and women in front of the city gate. Both young and old were in every respect handsome, stately people, except that their necks and heads were like those of cranes. Marching behind this multitude the watchers saw an army of the same creatures. Some wore swords, more carried bows, and all wore bright mail beneath their silk mantles.

The Crusaders were not frightened at the wondrous sight, but held the unusual beings in low esteem. "Let us remain here," said the duke, "where we can see all that they do. They will all come to this park, to the tables that hold the feast. They can't harm us, and we'll easily get back to the ship whether they wish it or not. One could slice through three of such bare, thin necks with one sword stroke."

Four elegantly clad warriors led the army that was now entering the city. Behind them strode a crane-man whose garments gleamed with many gems. He wore a silk tunic, a coat of silk and gold fabric, and a crown with sparkling jewels. Judging from their clothing, the two who followed him were highborn nobles. They led between them the most beautiful girl Ernst had ever seen. Her skin was whiter than snow; her hair reached to the ground; her form—enclosed in pure gold—was lovely beyond compare; her beautiful features were those of normal people. She was weeping without restraint.

After the girl was led into the city, all of the people crowded through the gates until no one, old or young, remained outside. Uttering strange sounds, they sang their native melodies as the king brought her straight to the enclosure with the many fine seats; the racket was deafening as the festivities began. One could see the girl's despair when she looked at those around her; the tears fell without ceasing down to her breast.

The lord high steward stood in front of the tables and assigned seats by pointing out chairs with a baton. He then sent servants to all, to pour wine for them and get them whatever they wanted: there was plenty of everything one could think of.

The king walked in state to his table, and at his side the steward seated the wretched girl. She and the king washed their hands in heavy gold basins, and chamberlains in splendid attire kneeled and offered them towels. The banquet deserved the highest praise.

When the duke and his companions heard the girl crying, they were moved with pity. "I'll never in my life be happy again," said Ernst, "if we can't think of some way to get this lovely woman away from here; my heart aches that she must suffer so."

"Prince," said one of his warriors, "Let us stay hidden here until the king leads her to his bedroom. We'll follow them, seize the lady, and take her away. We'll be outside the gate before they know it, and our comrades will rush to aid us there. We'll cover the lady with our shields and bring her safely to our ship." The duke was happy with the plan.

They didn't have to wait long until the king had finished eating. Then everyone stood up, and he went to the great hall. There was string music and singing, courtly dancing and folk dancing—all to honor the girl. But this entertainment didn't raise her spirits, so the king sent them away and led his bride to the beautiful chamber that was his bedroom. Only twelve of his men were with him when the six knights rushed into the room with their bare swords gleaming and cut down the king and all those with him but one, who managed to escape and spread the alarm.

Taking the girl by the hand, Duke Ernst hurried with his men from the palace and toward the city gate, but, before they could reach it, the way was blocked by a host of warriors. Holding up their shields before them and swinging their swords fiercely, five knights charged into the enemy while the duke protected the girl with his mail-clad body and his shield. The Bavarian blades did not miss the long, thin necks, and great numbers were beheaded as they cut a path to the gate. When the Crusaders found it barred, they put their backs to the wall and the duke sounded his horn. Then the enemy swordsmen drew back and the archers launched thousands of arrows; the knights' shields became so heavy that they had to cut them off with their swords.

Soon their companions arrived and hacked their way in through the gate, and all retreated toward the ship. Help had come barely in time, for some of the enemy had gone up on the parapets and were hurling down heavy stones. Once outside the wall there was no pursuit, and it seemed that the rescue of the girl was a success. But then there was a great shower of arrows coming not behind them from the city, but from their left; a second regiment of crane-men had arrived. Struck by one of the arrows, the beautiful girl screamed and fell. Ernst lifted her up and ran toward the ship while his men charged and quickly destroyed the new enemy force. Although they had won a great victory with few casualties, the Crusaders did not celebrate, for the beautiful girl was dead. They buried her with their fallen comrades by the sea, embarked, and set sail again.

The duke and his men had wandered for several years from one strange land and people to another when a second fierce storm drove them to the coast of the Holy Land. Here Ernst fought against the heathen with such success that his fame was carried back to Germany and the emperor by pilgrims. Otto had lost confidence in the count who had maligned his stepson and had begun to wonder if the latter might have been innocent of the charges brought against him. He therefore sent word to Ernst that the Imperial Diet would be meeting in Bamberg at Christmas time and that he would grant safe passage to the duke if he were to come there and plead his case before his peers. Ernst did so, was declared innocent, and was reconciled with his stepfather, who promptly gave him back his lands. Afterward the wanderer was prevailed upon to relate his many strange adventures to the assembled princes.

I thanked the good monk for his interesting tale, and we returned to the monastery. The next morning I went on to Nuremberg, a two-day journey. I was especially interested in seeing the Imperial Castle, built by a Saxon emperor and now a residence of the Swabian Hohenstaufens. In size and grandeur it surpassed my expectations; and the inner courtyard with its century-old linden tree was truly charming. I was told by a guard that King Philip happened to be there at the same time as I, but he did not volunteer to introduce us. Still elated at having finished my romance, I dared to wonder who would be remembered longer, the king or the poet. A day and a half later I was hurrying along the familiar rugged trail from Abenberg to Eschenbach. After a long absence I was home.

My first business concerned the primeval forest to the east of Eschenbach. For a modest annual fee, Duke Poppo had agreed to let the villagers clear a narrow strip, amounting to about fifty acres, along the north bank of the river and use it as a meadow. The peasants were pleased and at once began to measure off the boundaries of their future common. Several days later I had an unusual visitor, the hermit Giraldus, an old man who lived in the forest about a mile from the village. He had moved there when I was a child. On hearing of his presence, my father, as Count Poppo's representative, had sought him out to see if he was an illegal farmer on the count's land. "He has not cut down any trees," Sir Eberhard later told mother, "not even to build a shelter. So he has as much right to be there as the deer or the hares, which he does not trap but lives on plant roots and the nuts of the many walnut and beech trees in the forest."

Giraldus was quite distressed. "I shall lose my home," he lamented, "and I have no place to go. The peasants will cut down the trees for a pasture."

"I'll go back with you to your dwelling," I said, "and see what can be done."

The hermit's home was small and Spartan. A rock shelf formed the low ceiling of a shallow cave, that had been further enclosed by a stone wall for which clay had served as mortar. The bed consisted of an old blanket over a pile of dry grass; four flat stones, stacked one on top of another, served as a chair; a higher stack was his table; along the inner wall stood a bench made of the trunks of three saplings supported on each end by stones. This held all of the hermit's few utensils and a sack that contained his other possessions. "I have lived in this forest for twenty-seven years," said Giraldus. "It is my home. But this is its only cave, and I'll have to leave it."

"Don't worry," I told him. "When the peasants clear the land, there will be plenty of logs for a cabin. Before you leave here, they'll help you build one wherever you want." As I turned to go, I brushed against the sack on the bench and its contents spilled onto the floor. Among them was a splendid silk mantle on which a griffin was embroidered with gold thread. We stood there motionless: the hermit wide-eyed with terror, I in shocked surprise. It had been about twenty-seven years since a Prince Gerhart of Wittelsbach had been slain by a Count Hermann of Scheyern. The latter was declared a murderer and was outlawed, but he had never been caught. The emblem of the lords of Scheyern was a griffin.

"I don't know where you found that mantle," I said after a long pause, "but I think that you should get rid of it. Somcone might accuse you of stealing it."

"I'll do so at once," replied the old man. "At once!"

Sir Eberhard would not have needed to see the mantle to have guessed the identity of the hermit, but he made his own judgments and did not act on those of others. I thought it well to follow his example. The man who called himself Giraldus was relocated to another part of the forest, and I never saw him again. I believe that he died a few years later.

Two months after the completion of my romance, Baron Rupert invited a large number of nobles to Wildenberg to hear Karl read the manuscript. And, since the work was praised enthusiastically, I soon became rather famous and received more than a few requests to present it myself. I did not have a manuscript, but I had committed most of the verses to memory and had acquired enough skill at versifying to make up the others as I went along. As I did not need to follow a text, I could concentrate on acting, at which I admit to having considerable talent. I enjoyed these performances and was quite well paid for them.

About the end of June, in 1208, the report reached Eschenbach that King Philip had been murdered. I rode at once to Ansbach to learn the circumstances from Uncle Hugo, for, like many others, I assumed that the assassin was a supporter of Otto of Braunschweig, which would surely have led to renewed conflict between the Welf and Hohenstaufen camps. It is doubtful that all the facts concerning this tragic event have ever come to light, but the story the abbot told me then is probably closer to the truth than many that circulated during the decades that followed. According to Hugo, the murder had nothing to do with German or Empire politics but grew out of a more personal quarrel. Apparently Philip had promised to give his daughter in marriage to Count Otto of Wittelsbach because of the latter's prominent family, but, when he became aware of the count's unstable nature, he changed his mind. Although this deeply offended Otto, he avoided an open break with the king and sent an emissary to ask that Philip support his suit for the hand of the duke of Silesia's daughter. When this request was denied, Otto went to argue his case in person during the king's residence in Bamberg. On being again refused, he drew a dagger, slew Philip, and fled.

"This version of why the king was killed is based largely on rumor," admitted Hugo, "but it makes sense. At any rate there is no reason to connect the assassin with the Welfs. I'm glad of that, although there is still certain to be a struggle between them and the Hohenstaufens, and the prospects of the latter are not good. Philip was the last of Barbarossa's sons and his grandson Friedrich is only fourteen. I expect that Otto of Braunschweig will be Germany's next king and the head of the Holy Roman Empire." As usual, the abbot's prediction was correct. I have sometimes thought it most unfortunate that such talent should be buried in a monastery.

Castle Wartburg

Two years after the death of Philip, I received a second commission, one that kept me busy, with one interruption, for the next four years. I had ridden to Wertheim to make my annual report when Count Poppo told me that Hermann of Thuringia had the manuscript of a French romance and wanted me to put it into German verse. Otto of Braunschweig had brought it for Hermann when he returned to Germany from his Duchy of Aquitania, to which he had fled from Philip. "Otto is no lover of either romance or song," said Poppo, "but he knew that Hermann was, and I suppose he expected this present to help his campaign to become king of Germany. I wonder what the other electors were given. I've heard that he promised to renounce sovereignty over Italy in order to get Pope Innocence to proclaim him head of the Empire."

"Can you tell me anything about the romance?" I asked.

"Not much," replied the count. "Hermann said that it deals primarily with two battles in Southern France between Christians—led by a Count Willehalm—and Saracens at the time of Charlemagne's son Louis."

"Then it's something like Priest Konrad's tale of Roland," I suggested.

"Apparently so," replied the count. "You have composed the best of the Arthurian tales and now have the opportunity to outdo the good priest and produce the greatest of Crusade stories."

"If this manuscript is as long as the first was," I replied, "a German version would take several years, and going back and forth will be a problem, for Wartburg is nearly twice as far from Eschenbach as Wildenberg."

"It will be an experience that you should not miss," declared Poppo. "Not only will you be composing an excellent poem, but you will be a part of the liveliest cultural activity in all Germany and will observe at close range the workings of Empire politics. The knowledge you gain of the latter can perhaps be useful in preparing your romance." I told the count that, when convenient, he might inform Hermann that I would come in late October.

Then I journeyed home.

I found mother too weak to leave her bed. When she saw how distressed I was at her condition, she told me a story, one I had not heard before:

There was a painter who for gain worked hard at his trade and supported himself well from it. With love he forged his mind solidly to Our Lady, which could often be seen in the traits that he sought to portray. Once he was painting a mural high above a church altar, and in the scene appropriate likenesses of many Biblical figures appeared. With artistry and great care he painted the Holy Mary as beautiful as he possibly could. Then he began to sketch the devil and did not let him off easy, but used all of his art to make the form horribly misshapen. Because of this the devil became very bold with anger and appeared in flesh and blood on the high scaffold. "Aha!" he cried. "Now tell me! I'd like to know why you are so zealous with the lady's portrait, to paint her so carefully with loving tenderness, while you make me ugly, to say the least."

The good man was a little frightened, but he quickly took courage and then raged very abusively against the filthy creature: "You are truly so vile, so evil, and so detestable that anything which I could do to make you look worse would suit you very well. My Lady on the other hand is so virtuous, so beautiful, and so good that I shall make her as lovely as my skill allows. If I knew something more charming than I have painted here, I would add it to her in order to praise her as she deserves." When the devil flew into a rage and was about to throw him down to the flagstones far below, the good man began to cry to Our Lady. And just look! The picture of Mary on the wall stretched out its right hand and held him safely up. The devil fled hastily and left the man in peace.

"I too have faith in the Virgin," said mother, "and believe that she will protect me from evil. Whatever happens to me will be for my good." She died two weeks later, and the house felt empty for a long time. At first I thought that I would have to stay in Eschenbach to oversee the household activities and the commerce with the peasants—duties that mother had always performed—but my good wife at once showed full competence in these matters, and I decided to keep my agreement. Still there was much that I had to attend to before I could leave; I did not even have time to visit Abbot Hugo until the middle of October.

In spite of his eighty years, he was quite vigorous and, as always, was well-informed with respect to Empire politics. "Otto of Braunschweig may have a short reign as king and emperor," he told me. "I have heard that he now claims sovereignty over Italy. If this is so, I am almost certain that the pope will excommunicate him, which will greatly strengthen the hand of the Hohenstaufens. Young Friedrich may yet be emperor and your Count Hermann may once more change sides in this power struggle."

When I told him of my new project, the abbot had this to say: "Many military campaigns have been called Crusades—those of Charlemagne against the Saxons, of Otto the Great against the Slavs and Hungarians, of the kings of England, France, and Germany against the Saracens, to name a few—but the main purpose of all was to gain land and power, not to spread Christianity. I hope that your work will not attribute purely religious motives to your Crusaders; this is hypocrisy. The actions of Roland in Konrad's tale, for example, were no more Christian than those of his enemies. But you must stay here tonight and perform for us. Tell us about the amusing trials of Gawain. Serious times need light entertainment."

I promised to avoid hypocrisy in my new narrative and agreed to have Gawain amuse the monks with his wooing of the duchess. "If the wine is good," I added, "you'll also hear some new songs." I remember that day as if it were yesterday. The abbot and I talked all afternoon, about both the past and the present. He had much to say concerning my mother, his favorite niece, and his brother, my grandfather, who had died the previous winter. "Both were quiet revolutionists," he declared. "They examined all matters, whether social, political, or religious, from their own unique point of view and were uninfluenced by the opinions of others, living or dead. For them every day was the first day of creation."

"I was never really aware of this," I admitted. "I learned at an early age that all my mother's stories taught something, although I was seldom sure what it was. In fact, it often seemed to me that the apparent teaching of one contradicted the apparent teaching of another. But I was always too charmed by the stories and the way she told them to pay much attention to such things. Her father was for me a holiday figure, for whenever we visited at Abenberg, almost all work-day activities ceased and there was a festive celebration over which he presided. Indeed he may have affected my portrayal of King Arthur."

"I believe it," said the abbot, "and it is easy to see your father in Gahmuret. Eberhart too lived almost solely by his instincts, but they were good instincts that seldom if ever led him astray."

He had much to say about Germany's present situation: the relations between king and individual princes, the tensions between North and South, the struggle between Welfs and Hohenstaufens. "This last especially holds our attention," he said, "but it actually has only a temporary significance. The real struggle, the one that affects Germany's future, is that between pope and emperor. Will the ultimate authority of the secular institutions of the Holy Roman Empire rest in a German who has been elected by German princes or in an Italian who has been elected by Italian cardinals?"

That evening my portrayal of Gawain and his tyrannical ladylove evoked much laughter, as did my rendition of some new love song parodies. It was a happy evening. I felt, as always, that some magic charm rested in the monastery walls that would not let care or grief pass. Two days later I was on my way to Wartburg.

If it has been a good growing summer and the weather is pleasant, late October is the best time of the year in Franconia. With plenty of hay in the lofts, grain and beans in the bins, smoked pork hanging from the rafters, and cabbage and turnips in the cellars, the peasants can face the immediate future with confidence. All the towns and villages through which I passed were merrily celebrating their harvest festivals and honoring St. Oswald with colorful parades. On a meadow just outside of Ansbach a throng of dancers were springing gaily about to a lively tune, while a second, somewhat older, crowd sat under the trees and consumed new wine and onion cakes.

I stopped for a while at Ober Dachstettin and joined the onlookers of an amusing presentation of St. George's encounter with the dragon. A girl, closely pursued by a man with a dragon's mask, ran screaming into the circle of spectators. She fell and was about to be eaten when a man with the mask of a knight, mounted on the back of another man with a horse's head, charged at the dragon. A fierce battle ensued, and St. George was repeatedly knocked from his steed before he impaled the dragon with his spear.

A large field on the edge of Schweinfurt served as a sports arena with contesting runners, jumpers, archers, and wrestlers. Two professional entertainers were also there: a dancing bear and an acrobat who performed amazing feats on the ground and on a tightrope. What I found most exciting was a race between twelve youths on stilts; only six made it to the finish line without falling.

Every day of the journey I encountered two or three parades in which all the inhabitants of a village decked themselves out with sheaves of grain and marched to and from a shrine to honor St. Oswald. I have often wondered about this custom. "According to Church writings," Abbot Hugo once told me, "Oswald was a Celtic king who defeated and converted the heathen West Saxons of England." And according to a legend that I heard recited at Wertheim, he sailed overseas and abducted a heathen princess—with her help and that of a talking raven—but, when he brought her home and married her, an angel appeared to tell him that he was not to have any carnal intercourse with his bride. "You must keep a tub of cold water by your bed," said the heavenly messenger, "and spring into it when afflicted by sensual desire." We learn from this that God has a sense of humor, and perhaps that explains why He put a former king, who knew nothing of sowing and reaping, in charge of peasant husbandry.

Although I shared the joy of those I saw along the road, I could not forget the abbot's premonition of war. Nor could I forget that these happy villagers and townspeople had no walls, magic or otherwise, to protect them from its fury.

A few miles beyond Schweinfurt I overtook a knight, who also was traveling north, and, as he seemed a pleasant fellow, I was pleased when he suggested that we ride on together. Since we were abreast of Meiningen toward evening, he proposed that we leave the main road, cross the river, and camp on a pretty meadow just outside of the town. At the entrance to the bridge stood a broad board that displayed the likeness of the devil in flaming red—horns, tail, goat's foot, and all. "Do you know why that painting is there?" I asked my companion.

"Certainly," he replied. "This is 'The Devil's Bridge.' "

"And how did it get that name?" I inquired.

"I'll tell you tonight," he promised. "But let us cross ourselves before riding onto it, because there may be some truth to the story." Later, when we had eaten and were sitting by the fire, I reminded him of the bridge. He took a long drink of the wine we had gotten from a local merchant and began:

Centuries ago, when Meiningen was growing from a small village into a town, both the citizens and their lord, Count Igor, decided that they should have a bridge across the Werra because the water was often too high or too low for them to use the ferry. They struggled for five years in vain with the construction. Arches and piers collapsed for no apparent reason, were rebuilt, and collapsed again. The project was on the verge of being abandoned when Master Venefica appeared before the count with a proposal.

Venefica was a learned magician who had acquired great powers, supposedly from the study of Latin and Arabic works. With his vast knowledge of minerals and herbs, he made salves that could cure almost any malady of man or beast; he read in the stars many events of both past and future; and he could tell from examining a fowl's entrails where lost cattle had wandered. These were just a few of the accomplishments that caused him to be highly regarded, even though many suspected him of witchcraft.

"My esteemed lord," said the magician, "it looks as though the devil himself is behind the trouble with the bridge. If you were inclined to offer him something that he prizes, I'm sure that he would not only let it be completed, but might even aid the builders. Some of the finest bridges in Germany were constructed with his help, and both you and the town need one. Even I, your humble servant, would be glad to have a bridge, for I live on the other side of the river."

"And what price does the devil demand?" asked Igor.

"Just a single soul, no more, my lord," replied Venefica, "that of the first man or woman to cross the bridge. In return you would have a structure that will last for centuries."

"But I can't condemn anyone to eternal damnation," objected the count. "It would be a sin that could cost me my own soul. No, we'll just have to make do with the ferry."

"My lord," said a wise old counselor named Adam, "perhaps it would be well to consider the matter for a few days before making a decision. Your present and future welfare and that of the townspeople are at stake." Igor reluctantly agreed, and asked the magician to return in a week. "If you will trust me, my lord," said the counselor after Venefica's departure, "I shall see that we have a bridge and that the devil gets nothing but what is already his."

"I trust you," replied the count. "Take charge of the matter."

When the magician next appeared, he was received by Adam, who said, "I have drawn up two copies of a contract that reads as follows: "If Sir Satan will permit a bridge to be built here across the Werra and guarantee that it will last for five hundred years, he shall have the soul of the first person, and no other, who crosses it." Both copies have been signed by the count, who asks that one be returned with the devil's signature. Can you arrange it? If all goes well, you will receive ten gold marks."

"I'll take care of everything," replied Venefica delighted. "In a heathen book I read an incantation that will cause an imp to appear. He will get his master's name on the contract and bring it to me."

As soon as the count saw the contract with the devil's signature, he ordered construction to begin, and the work went forward with almost unbelievable speed. Solid foundations for the piers were discovered at once, and every stone fit so precisely that mortar was hardly necessary. In a month's time the bridge was finished.

Hearing that it was completed, the magician set out in haste to collect his pay but, when he reached the bridge, he was stopped by a courtier disguised as a peasant. "Take care, sir, don't step on the bridge!" cried the latter. "Only five minutes ago a peddler tried to cross, but when he put his foot on the other side, he screamed horribly and vanished."

"There is no danger, my good man," laughed the magician, and hurried over the river to his doom.

"Do you believe the tale?" I asked my companion.

"Let us say that I do not reject it," he replied. "Did you look closely at the bridge? After standing there for centuries, it is still in excellent condition, and no one has ever heard of its being repaired. That is not natural."

The next morning we went on together for a few miles before my companion turned off toward Schmalkalden, and two days later I rode into Eisenach. A tournament was in progress on the field below the castle, but it seemed to me that the prevailing spirit there was more businesslike than festive, as if the participants were practicing military manoeuvers rather than competing for a prize. I also noticed that all the pennants displayed were those of Count Hermann's Thuringian vassals. Apparently none of his Saxon vassals were present. "Why is that?" I wondered as I rode up to the castle.

Wartburg was built above the town of Eisenach by a remote ancestor of Count Hermann who, for some forgotten reason, was called Ludwig the Springer. It is a massive structure that straddles a narrow ridge with steep sides at the northwest edge of the Thuringian Forest. Although the castle looks as if it could withstand any assault, it is quite beautiful and after a fashion not characteristic of German castles. Crossing the drawbridge and passing through the gate, one enters the armory, beyond which are the private living quarters of the count. The stairway to the second floor leads to the courtroom, then to the Singers' Hall with its stage and auditorium, and beyond this is the chapel and the library. The entire third floor is taken up by the Great Hall. Smaller buildings inside the walls house guest rooms, retainers' quarters, kitchen, stables, and the like.

I have heard that the castle was erected on the site of a stronghold built as an outpost by Charlemagne's armies during his wars against the Saxons. At that time, so the story goes, the northern half of the Thuringian Forest was inhabited only by a race of dwarfs who mined silver and gold, which they wrought into fine ornaments that were sold in distant lands. The dwarfs greatly resented the intrusion of the emperor's Franks and made their passage difficult by destroying their bridges, felling trees and digging trenches across their roads, or sending down rock slides and avalanches upon their troops and supply trains as these passed below bluffs or bare mountain slopes.

According to some of the tales, the dwarfs at times were most ingenious and resolute in their efforts to discourage these foreigners from passing through their land. One Frank chronicler wrote: "No deed was too evil for those demons! Having noted that our troops often camped along the banks of a certain stream, they built a dam across it further up the mountain, thus creating a rather large lake. Then one night when several thousand warriors were sleeping below, they broke the dam, and the resulting torrent swept away the entire encampment: men, horses, and supplies. They surely are agents of the devil." When I read this, it occurred to me that it might have been a beaver dam that broke.

Although the dwarfs were not in league with the Saxons, the latter were greatly aided by such actions, which explains why it took Charlemagne so long to subjugate them. There was little the Franks could do about the dwarfs. They were so adept at disappearing into the undergrowth or into their many tunnels that they were thought to have the power to make themselves invisible, and their bold harassment of the emperor's forces led some to believe them possessed of superhuman strength. In after years most of the dwarfs left, perhaps because the richest veins of gold and silver had been mined. But even today, so I have been told, the traveler through the forest will sometimes hear the tapping of their hammers.

I announced my arrival to the count's steward, who took me at once to Hermann's scribe. The latter, a young priest named Albert, led me to the library and showed me the French manuscript. It was not bound but was splendidly illuminated. "The manuscript appears to be incomplete," said Albert. "Some leaves seem to be missing at the end, but this should be no problem for you. That was also the case with the source of the Parzival story that you finished up so well. How good is your French? Should I translate the manuscript for you?"

"My French is adequate," I assured him. "but as yet my handwriting is not. If we were to meet here for an hour each evening, you could write down the verses that I compose during the day." We agreed on this and went to the great hall where, so I had heard, there was never any lack of entertainment. We were particularly fortunate on this occasion, for Walther of Vogelweide, who had arrived just two day before me, sang a large number of his political songs. The one I liked best was more patriotic than political, and, since it is surely forgotten by now, you shall hear me sing it:

> Welcome and with all good cheer
> him who brings you stories; I am he.
> All the other tales told here
> were an empty wind. Now come hear me.
> First give me my reward,
> if it satisfies,
> things I'll tell, perhaps, to open wide your eyes.
> See what gifts you can afford!
>
> German ladies shall embrace
> news of such a nature that they may
> better charm us with their grace.

That I'll do for no excessive pay.
What shall be the fee?
I can't reach so high;
I'll be modest if the ladies be not shy
and will greet me tenderly.

I have travelled far and wide,
have traversed the best of lands indeed;
may misfortune be my guide,
should I make my erring heart concede
that it was impressed
by their foreign ways.
Well, what would I gain by false and empty praise?
German manners are the best!

From the Elbe to the Rhine,
eastward all the way to Hungary,
there the fairest beauties shine
that this wanderer ever hopes to see.
He who understands
lovely forms as well
as I, would swear, by God, our peasant girls excel
fine ladies in all other lands.

German men are all refined,
angels can't surpass the women here;
who thinks otherwise is blind,
so, at least to me, it would appear.
He who seeks in vain
culture, love, and light,
should come into a land where all of these unite.
May I evermore remain!

I admit that Sir Walther praises us a bit too highly, but, as everyone agrees, it is the nature of poetry to overstate the truth. In any case, a race that thinks well of itself may sometimes be inclined to show its cultural superiority by its actions.

In the next few days I learned that court life in Castle Wartburg was truly chaotic. The count had no guest list. Any young nobleman who became bored at home could pitch his tent on the field below and take part in the afternoon and evening festivities. Indeed, after a scheduled program in the great hall, a large part of the audience often would remain there and provide its own entertainment with singing and dancing to all hours of the night. Some were often found sleeping on the floor when the servants came to set up tables there for the morning meal. I was assigned to the large bedroom that accommodated male guests of the lesser nobility, and, since these too were a rather noisy lot, I got permission from the steward to move my cot to the library, where I would be working. This was a small room off of the chapel and it was quiet except during morning mass. When Walther learned of my move, he asked leave to join me, for the constant turmoil disturbed him even more than it did me.

We were congenial companions. When we were not working—he, composing songs; I, with my version of Willehalm's adventures—we talked about our experiences. He had traveled much more widely than I and had performed at all of the larger courts of the German lands. He much preferred that of Duke Leopold in Vienna, but he could never be more than a visitor there since Sir Reinmar was firmly established as the court poet. I felt sorry for Walther. As the younger son of a minor nobleman, he had no fief of his own and therefore, despite his great fame, was homeless. I was greatly pleased some years later to hear that he had been granted a fief by Emperor Friedrich.

I was amazed at how easily he could turn a personal experience, however trivial, into a song. For example, a minor accident occurred during a hunting party a few weeks after Walther arrived at Wartburg. A brash and careless young nobleman named Gerhart Atze shot at a deer they were chasing and hit Walther's horse. The arrow inflicted only a slight wound and nothing would have come of the affair if Gerhart had apologized. Instead he insisted that Walther was at fault for coming between him and the deer. That very night Walther composed a little song with a lively tune that became very popular at once. Gerhart became so tired of hearing everyone singing it that he left Wartburg and never returned. These are the words:

Sir Gerhart Atze shot my horse
at Eisenach quite dead.
My grievances I now shall lay
before our mutual lord.
The beast was worth a lot, of course,
but just hear what he said
when it appeared he'd have to pay
the debt that he'd ignored.
He speaks of pain and need
and said my horse indeed
was brother to the steed
that bit his thumb, and both
had caused him grief thereby.
I swear with two hands high
all that is just a lie.
Who here will take my oath.

It is ironical that Gerhart Atze has perhaps gained lasting fame by the incident. I never heard of him again, but after forty years the song was still well known.

I spent the first two weeks at the castle reading through the French manuscript and could see that it would be necessary to stay closer to my source than I had done with the Parzival story, for this was not legend but history. The two battles that made up the core of the narrative really occurred, so I was told. They were fought by the Christian French and the Mohammedan Saracens in Southern France during the reign of Louis the Pious, Charlemagne's son. And that not only Count Willehalm, now St. Willehalm, but also certain other characters in the story took part in this historical struggle is attested by other records. Still I did not think I would be reduced to mere translation, for there were many elements of the account before me that could be reshaped to my wishes.

One of the these was the family relationships of the heroine. The manuscript told of the Christian Willehalm, held prisoner by a Saracen king, being set free by the king's wife, who fled with him to his border stronghold, where they married. Her father and former husband promptly collected a great army and followed in order to avenge the offense to their honor and bring her back. I determined to develop the tragic situation of a woman torn between her new faith and the man she adored on the one hand and the former husband whom she respected and the father she loved on the other; she was to plead for tolerance. I also intended to portray the battles not merely as great conflicts but as struggles that threatened the very existence of the Empire and all Christendom. There was much that could be done with this French story and I was eager to begin.

During the following months I found that the one quiet haven in the castle, the library, was in itself a distraction that often kept me from my work. Although I learned to read French and German while composing my Parzival romance, it was a skill that I had not used since, for I had no books. Abbot Hugo was my only kinsman who had books and his were all in Latin. But here there were dozens of bound manuscripts. Some contained stories I had heard read, like Heinrich of Veldeke's tale of Aeneas and Hartmann of Aue's romances about Erec and Iwein; others held works I knew only by reputation.

One of the latter was the romance about Tristan and Isolde, by a citizen of Strassburg named Gottfried. I read it at once. Although incomplete, it is a great work, but fortunately not to everyone's taste; society would soon collapse if we all valued sexual love above loyalty. I believed that I detected in Gottfried's comments on German poets an allusion to my style that was not complimentary. Well, if he needs an interpreter to learn what I mean to say, so much the worse for him.

A few of the manuscripts contained tales by poets of whom I

had never heard. One of these was an Eilhart of Oberge, who also told of Tristan and Isolde; another was Bligger of Steinach, who recounted a long series of tales about King Arthur's knights. Both works were interesting and at times highly amusing. There was no great need to hurry with this Willehalm work, I decided, for I might never see such a library again.

As I remember, it was about Christmas of that year, 1210, that the news reached Wartburg that Pope Innocence had excommunicated Emperor Otto and had demanded that the German princes choose another king. There was little excitement at the court, for Count Hermann had apparently anticipated this action and had decided on the course he would take. His position was not easy, for his powerful vassals had long been divided on Welf versus Hohenstaufen hegemony—the Saxons supporting the former, the Thuringians, the latter—and, if Otto were forced to abdicate as king and emperor, his obvious successor would be Barbarossa's grandson Friedrich. The latter, who had been king of Sicily since age four, was now sixteen and enjoyed the favor of the pope.

After the death of his father, Friedrich's mother had appointed Innocence as his guardian. And shortly before the excommunication of Otto, the pope had declared his ward to be of age and had greatly increased the youth's stature by arranging a marriage with Konstanze, the daughter of the king of Aragon and the widow of the king of Hungary. Well aware of all this, Hermann was certain that Friedrich would be king and emperor and thought it would do no harm if he, duke of Saxony and count of Thuringia, were to get some of the credit for bringing this about.

In the spring therefore Hermann arranged for the German princes to meet in Nuremberg, where he convinced a majority to depose Otto and elect Friedrich as their king. But Hermann's Saxon vassals promptly turned on their lord. I was glad to be able to say that my duties as local steward for Count Poppo as well as the need to oversee my own fief, required my presence in Eschenbach. Unlike my father, who enjoyed combat for its own sake, I have always wanted to choose my quarrels on the basis of their merit and my personal advantage, and I saw no pressing reason at the time to fight for a man who once had tried to starve me, even though he subsequently became a fairly generous employer.

His summer was livelier and, I assume, less enjoyable than mine. I learned from Abbot Hugo that the Saxon nobles had quickly occupied several of Hermann's towns and driven him back when he tried to recapture them; moreover three of his castles were under siege and one of them had been taken. All-in-all the count's authority had vanished in Saxony and had been damaged in Thuringia. He got little or no aid from the others who had voted for Friedrich, for they had to deal with rebellion or the threat of rebellion in their own lands. Apparently support for Otto, or opposition to the pope, was stronger and more widespread than had been anticipated.

But in Eschenbach all this was distant rumor. Indeed all Franconia appeared to be free of tension and dissent. The lords were waiting to see what Friedrich would do, the peasants were tending their cattle and crops, and my wife was too busy preparing for the wedding of her daughter to a handsome young vassal of the count of Ansbach to be concerned with either Empire politics or the local economy. When I was not busy with the affairs of my fief, I engaged in jousting and swordplay with my fifteen-year-old son, who was to become a page at Wertheim in the fall. He had a fine voice, but had no talent for composing either verse or melodies.

I did not return to Wartburg in the fall. With all of the fighting going on in Thuringia, according to reports, it seemed most unlikely that I could have gotten there in any case. "Count Hermann won't miss me," I told my wife, "he has enough warfare of his own to deal with and won't be greatly concerned about battles that took place four hundred years ago." The harvest festival was not quite as merry as usual because lack of rain in August had reduced the yield of grain and hay. But there was still some of both from the previous year and the fall cabbage and turnips had done well, so the peasants were not worried about the winter.

Nothing important occurred during this stay at Eschenbach, and I remember it mainly because of a conversation I had with the village priest, the one for whom I had sung as a boy. We had finished eating—he frequently had dinner with us on Sundays—and were discussing various trivial village affairs when I happened to ask him why he became a priest.

"That is a good question," he replied, "for I was the elder son of a knight with a hereditary fief that would have come to me. The fact is that I became a priest because of a dream, or perhaps a vision. Do you attach any significance to such things?"

"Not as prophesy," I replied. "I believe that, when they are meaningful, they usually are so only in retrospect. Dreams seldom alter the course of events and are therefore a poor guide for action. You may remember that the death of Siegfried was foretold in a dream, but Kriemhild's attempts to avert it were in vain. This, I think, is nearly always the case. But tell me about your dream." This is the story I heard:

Once, on my sixteenth birthday, while riding along a familiar highway, I suddenly realized that I must have unknowingly turned off onto a side road, for everything appeared quite strange. At the same time I heard sounds of battle and spurred my steed forward to see what was happening. I came upon a company of knights, all decked out in shining white armor, who were being attacked by a long spear that hovered above a white horse. I could not see anyone wielding the spear as it charged here and there, cutting down the frightened and helpless knights. When all were dead, the bodies burst into flame and the horse with the bloody spear turned away.

Despite my horror, I followed its trail and soon came upon a beautiful maiden with a stick who was trying to drive large birds away from the fresh wounds of an ugly, chained giant. But she could not save him, and they stripped off his flesh with such ravenous fury that they quickly tore him open, gnawed away at his heart, and divided his entrails between them. I did not stop to question the maiden, because I was afraid of losing track of the spear.

A short time later I witnessed another remarkable scene. Mounted on a huge, green beast that had a long, sharp horn on its forehead, was an old woman who wore richly embellished clothing. Her face was yellow and deathlike, and her gray hair fell down over her hips. In her left hand was a strong hemp rope with which she had bound a tall, naked Moor who ran along by her side and screamed pitiably as she beat him cruelly with a whip. I was distressed at his cries and, had I not been in such haste, would gladly have interceded for him.

Just as I emerged from a forest, a knight galloped toward me in full flight. He wore black armor and in his right hand held a woman's head by the braids. A knight in red chased after him, calling loudly, but vainly, for him to stop; in less than a minute both were out of sight.

I then saw before me in a meadow a splendid palace that was surrounded by a beautiful wall—at least twelve fathoms high—of thin, transparent crystal. From within came many sounds of merriment, expressed in sweet and joyous song. Then a frightful peasant, naked and black as a raven, came striding out of the forest and across a broad field. He was a good six fathoms tall and was swinging a rough, steel club some thirty paces long before him as he came. The peasant rushed up to the wall, swung his club back over his shoulder and struck such a dreadful blow that the wall was shattered: it fell to the ground and burst into flames. The pretty maidens inside, who had been entertaining themselves, became silent, then collapsed and began to smolder. When the palace was burning inside and out, the peasant entered and pushed the bodies into the fire with his club.

I rode on, through another forest and out onto a blooming heath. There stood a beautiful and richly dressed boy, who had suffered the misfortune of having an arrow shot through both of his eyes. His legs were tied together and he was firmly bound to a bed with two iron chains. In his hand he held a fan that would destroy the glow of the flowers when it was waved, for the breeze that came from it was like fire. He was using it to fan a maiden who lay before him on the bed. She was dead. To one side lay a knight, black as a Moor, who had a large wound through his heart, and a spear fragment a yard long with a red banner was still sticking in him.

Up on the hill ahead, I got a brief glimpse of the white horse and beyond it saw a castle with four tall towers. As I approached, the gates opened and the drawbridge came down, but no one was there. Entering, I dismounted, tied my steed, and walked to a fine palace nearby. Since the door was open, I went in and found myself in a large hall with a bed at one end. In the bed lay a very old man and beside him stood a beautiful lady who was giving him blood to drink from a golden goblet. When the old man saw me, he called out my name and I awoke.

"This dream or vision," continued my guest, "was as real as any other experience I have had, and it left me, still a boy, badly shaken. I recounted it to my parents, who did not take the matter lightly, but went with me to the parish priest in hope of learning what, if anything, the dream meant. He interrupted now and then with questions as I told it. Then he said: 'I believe I understand everything but the end. With the exception of the old man, the people you saw were suffering in life and in purgatory because of evil. If the dream brings a message to you, and I believe it does, it is that you should devote your life to lessening this suffering.' I was convinced that he was right and became a novice at once."

"It was indeed a strange dream," I said, "and Eschenbach is grateful for it. But let me venture an interpretation of the last scene. Suppose the old man at the end called out his own name, that he was actually you at the end of your journey. And suppose the lady was the Virgin Mary administering the last rites with wine that was also blood."

"I hope that is correct," replied the priest. "I should have known that a poet would find a solution to the mystery. Perhaps we should go over the dream more carefully sometime so that you can interpret all the details."

In the spring I once more had an active role in Empire politics. Count Poppo sent messengers to all of his able-bodied vassals in our region, directing us to join the forces of King Friedrich. He had gathered an army in Italy and was now on his way to put down all insurrection in Germany. Within two weeks we were to assemble in Nuremberg and wait for him there. When I rode up, the plain along the banks of the Pegnitz was already covered with hundreds of tents; knights from all over Franconia had gathered there.

Five days later the Imperial armies arrived. I had never beheld such a sight before. The column stretched out along the road and vanished beyond the horizon. First came the Italians, displaying the Imperial banner and led by a company of at least a hundred trumpeters; the blast was deafening. The second army was made up of Swabians; the third of Easterners: Austrians, Styrians, Carinthians, Salzburgers, and Tyrolese; then came the Bavarians. Each army was preceded by its own company of ear-splitting trumpeters, and every company displayed its own colorful standard. If this mighty host had marched around the city, its walls would have fallen like those of Jericho. And these were not all of Friedrich's warriors in Germany; another force, so I heard, was moving down the Rhine.

Leaving Nuremberg, the main body of troops proceeded slowly northward as smaller detachments of one hundred to a thousand knights rode to east and west, asking the members of the resident nobility why they had not contributed to the Emperor's army as requested. These detachments were always larger when they returned than when they left, and many knights who had expected to support Otto found themselves in Friedrich's host. We did not encounter enemy troops until we entered Thuringia and these retreated before us. The Saxon troops that had besieged Hermann's castles and occupied his towns left before we arrived, which enabled the count to put a Thuringian army at Friedrich's disposal.

In Saxony our supply trains frequently came under attack by companies of hit and run cavalry, but the chief struggles took place when we stormed castles and other fortified positions. Some of the Saxon strongholds were so inaccessible that our vastly superior numbers meant little. These had to be starved into surrender. The war dragged on for two years before Otto's forces were completely crushed and he retired to Aquitania.

Then I returned to Wartburg and resumed work on the Willehalm story. I had left my hero in dire straits. In the first battle against the Saracens he had lost his army of twenty thousand men—including his nephew, the heroic Vivianz—and his castle, Orange, was under siege. Now he had to leave its defense to his wife and hurry to King Louis's unsympathetic court in Laon to beg for help. I did not envy him this mission.

The atmosphere at Wartburg had changed noticeably during my absence. There was still plenty of entertainment: dances, readings of romances, singer performances, and occasional tournaments, but the entertainment was not as lavish, the guests not as numerous, and their spirits not as boisterous. Perhaps the change reflected the count's financial losses during the rebellion, but it seemed to me that he lacked the boundless energy for which he was famous. Walther was gone, of course, but another had taken his place, a Herbort of Fritzlar, who also had been commissioned to translate a French manuscript.

Herbort was a well-educated man of about twenty-five. He had studied Latin at the monastery school in Fritzlar and had learned French in Paris while serving as the scribe of a Hessian nobleman who spent two years there. Herbort too had been a part of the Imperial army and had been released just a week or two before I was.

"What is your story about?" I asked.

"Mainly about the Trojan War," he replied. "Count Hermann wanted it translated to serve as an introduction to Heinrich of Veldeke's tale of Aeneas."

"It's quite an introduction," I observed, looking at the heavy volume. "It must weigh forty pounds. Apparently it was a long war."

"Ten years," he said, "but that is only the middle part. The manuscript begins with Jason's journey for the golden fleece and ends when Ulysses finally reaches his homeland. There are over thirty thousand verses, but, if I get tired of it, I can shorten the tale. Ulysses won't mind if I get him back to Ithaca several years earlier."

Herbort was a satirical fellow, and I have often wondered how he treated his Greek and Trojan heroes, but I never found out. While at Wartburg, I had no time to read such a long work, and later on, in Eschenbach, it was not available. Herbort was also handsome and single, and all of the maids-in-waiting were much taken with him, but their fathers were not. "It is all very well," thought the latter, "to be learned, talented, and charming, but what wealth does he have? Apparently none."

It was not just the maidens, some of the married ladies showed considerable interest in Herbort. One to such an extent that her jealous husband, a visiting nobleman named Volmar, accused him before the count of making improper advances to his wife. I was with Herbort when he went to Hermann and swore that he had not. The husband thereupon declared that he should be forced to prove the truth of his oath by undergoing the ordeal by fire, that is, by carrying a red-hot iron in his bare hand without being burned. Herbort countered by offering to prove it by combat. In reply, Volmar maintained that it would be beneath his dignity to cross swords with a scribe, who, though he had served in the army, had done so as a squire, not as a knight.

At this point, I reminded the count that I was a knight and the son of a renowned warrior, and was well qualified to represent my friend by fighting in his stead. The count, who liked to watch a good fight, at once agreed. But he was disappointed. Volmar would not accept my proposal, maintaining that his quarrel was only with "the scribe," and the following day he and his wife departed. Later Herbort told me in confidence that an "improper advance" had indeed been made, but that it had come from the lady. Count Hermann, who apparently knew the lady quite well, may have suspected as much. Herbort remained at Wartburg two years longer than I. When I last heard of him, he was serving a Thuringian nobleman and his family as scribe and tutor.

Of all the many famous people that ever lived or visited the celebrated court of Count Hermann, none achieved such extensive and lasting renown as a little girl who had come during my absence. This was Elizabeth, the daughter of King Andreas of Hungary, who at the age of four was betrothed to Hermann's son, Ludwig, and was raised from then on at Wartburg. She was a serious and pious child—I never saw her smile or laugh—who apparently even at such an early age, had been greatly influenced by her mother's sister, St. Hedwig. She insisted on attending all church services and on leaving in the offering box every piece of jewelry that was given her.

As she is remembered primarily for the miraculous healings caused after her death by her relics, I might be permitted a brief digression concerning her life after I left Wartburg. Since I maintained some ties with the court there for many years, I know more than most about her subsequent history. At fourteen she married Ludwig, who by then was Count Ludwig. Although her generous gifts to aid the poor and the sick, made it necessary for his court to get along rather frugally—quite unlike that of his father—Ludwig apparently did not object, and the two lived happily until his death while on a Crusade.

This tragedy was followed by another trial when her brother-in-law, Count Heinrich Raspe drove Elizabeth and her children from Wartburg, but the Thuringian nobles objected so strongly that she was allowed to return and was granted a sizable income. She refused subsequent offers of marriage, eventually moved from the castle to a small house below it, and gave everything she had to establish a hospital for the care of the sick and needy. She then supported herself by sewing. According to legend, Elizabeth performed miracles also during her lifetime, some even as a child. I heard of one of the latter while at Wartburg, but I did not witness it.

A knight had been hunting with his falcon and returned with a hare. The five-year-old Elizabeth was playing by the gate when he entered and, catching sight of the hare hanging from his belt, cried out in pity: "Oh the poor thing! Please, let me have it." Since no one ever refused any request of the pretty little girl, the knight untied the animal and laid it at her feet. Weeping, she stroked it gently and exclaimed: "Oh how I wish you were alive!" At this, so I was told, the hare leaped to its feet and ran away. At the time no one thought it a miracle; everybody laughed at the knight for being deceived by a hare that played dead and thereby escaped.

If I had been able to compose freely, I would have given Willehalm a better reception at Laon and would not have had him treat his sister, the queen, so roughly, but one must be cautious about altering history. At any rate, the hero's father, a mighty prince, immediately supported him and convinced the king and others to help, so that Willehalm could ride back to Orange with a large army. He also took Rennewart, one of the king's kitchen boys with him. This was a captive Saracen who, unknown to Willehalm and to himself, was his wife's brother and the son of his chief antagonist, Terramer. The boy, who was immensely strong, carried with him a great iron bar to use as a weapon against Willehalm's enemies.

I suppose that the popularity of the work has been largely due to the two great battles, but I was more interested in that which came between them: especially Gyburg's grief at being responsible for the deaths of thousands of valiant men, both Christian and heathen; the dialogue between Gyburg and her father concerning religion; and her appeal to the Christian princes to treat defeated Saracens kindly. I included this plea for religious tolerance in order to counter the excessive zeal that often is a part of the Crusading spirit and, since it was usually omitted by those who presented my romance to the public and was therefore almost unknown, I shall repeat some of it:

"If you vanquish the heathens," she admonished Willehalm's troops, "behave as true Christians. Treat them with chivalry, for they are God's creatures. Remember that the first man whom God created was a heathen and that Elijah and Enoch too were heathens, also Noah, who was able to save himself in the ark. Truly, one may likewise call Job a heathen, but God still did not reject him. Think of the three kings—Kaspar, Melchior, and Balthasar—who were heathens, but were surely not lost, for God Himself received His first gifts from them, if we do not consider the milk from His mother's breast. So not every heathen must be lost.

"We also know that all children born since Eve's time were heathens, even those with baptized mothers. In short, we all were once heathens. It is naturally painful for every Christian to know that his children are destined by God the Father for destruction, but we also believe that, should they die unbaptized, He will have mercy on them just as He has always done with the heathens. Whatever they have done to you, you should remember that God does not condemn them, although they took His life. Be merciful therefore if God grants you the victory."

I had gotten this far in my romance by late spring when I set out for Eschenbach. I went by way of Wertheim because it was rumored that Count Poppo was seriously ill, and I wanted to see him once more. He had always been most kind to me and had frequently expressed his satisfaction with my service to him. Although the count could not leave his bed, he received me and we talked for nearly an hour about my father and the time I had lived there as his page. "Those were the days," he said as I left him, "neither Germany nor the Empire has ever recovered from the death of old Barbarossa. Although he had his troubles down in Italy, he kept the peace up here, and we all prospered by it. He lived as an emperor should: I was one of the fifty thousand guests who attended the knighting festival he held for his sons in Mainz. There has been nothing like it since." These were almost his last words, for he went to sleep soon afterwards and never awakened.

I stayed on for several days in order to attend the funeral ceremony and to discuss my fief and duties with my new liegelord, Poppo the Younger. The old count was interred in a marble casket that was placed in an alcove which he had added to the chapel some years earlier for this purpose. His son told me that there would be no change with regard to my fief. With this assurance I departed for home.

When I stopped at the Ansbach monastery a week later, I was shocked to find that the funeral of Abbot Hugo was then taking place. It was a grievous loss to me, not only because I was very fond of my great uncle, but also because I had so often sought his advice. His death was a forceful reminder of the importance of the written word. I had always been greatly impressed by his vast knowledge and the lucid manner in which he could express it. Now it was gone, and I knew that when I and his other younger friends—one might call them disciples—were dead, it would be entirely forgotten, for he recorded nothing but routine matters concerning the monastery. Yet I hoped that at least one bit of his learning and wisdom would never die: the tolerance plea of Gyburg, which was based largely on some of his random comments.

My mother's case was similar. She was the greatest storyteller I have ever heard or read, but she could not write and I have never been able to retell her tales successfully. There was something about her style that I could never reproduce. So it is that, despite her genius, she will achieve no renown unless my poor rendering of two of her stories can win it. Only the written word can make one immortal.

Hugo was interred in the monastery's wine cellar. This large space, originally intended for a crypt, had also been used to store wine. But after some two hundred years it housed so many caskets that there was hardly enough room for the wine. From that time on, therefore, the deceased monks were buried in a graveyard outside the walls. And now, over two more centuries later, the cellar received another stone casket. Hugo had requested this, and some long forgotten monk had been removed to make room. "It gets so cold and damp outside," he said. "I would never be comfortable there." The brothers were happy to oblige him.

When I arrived at Eschenbach, I found the village greatly upset. A wandering cleric had been going about the region casting out devils and the peasants were convinced that the devils had moved into their cattle, which were acting very strangely. They feared that the milk would be spoiled, perhaps even poisonous, and that the offspring of the cows, sheep, and goats would be deformed. They had gotten no help from the village priest, who doubted that the beasts were devil-possessed and confessed that he could do nothing about it if they were.

"It was a long winter," he told me when I went to see him, "and the snow was late in leaving the pastures. Cattle always race about after they have been confined for a long time. No one would have thought anything about it, had it not been for that charlatan."

"You may be right," I replied, "but we need to get rid of these devils whether they are present or not. I have a plan, and you must help me."

Calling a meeting of all the villagers, I said, "This situation is not unusual and has often been successfully handled in Thuringia. Bring all your animals together, line them up, and I'll show you what is done there. The devils will be driven out, but sometimes it is several days before the cattle quiet down."

I had an old cow of mine killed and its blood collected into a pail. Then the priest and I went down the row of cattle. Going from one to the other, I daubed each with the blood while the priest made the sign of the cross over it and murmured his "in nomine patris. . . ." The devils were thereby exorcised; I knew that the milk would be good and the newborns would be flawless, and I was proud of my solution. "Little is gained by denial," Abbot Hugo once told me. "If you want to influence people, you must start with what they believe." But while the cattle, that had been almost unmanageable, were being driven back to the pasture, they were as calm and slow-moving as a team of tired oxen! No one but the priest and I was surprised.

That summer I noticed once more the encroachment of trade on the economy of the village. Engelmar, our leather-maker and shoemaker had died during the winter, and the son to whom he had taught the craft went to Ansbach to practice it. So whoever wanted shoes had to go there to get them. The situation was nearly as bad with a few other products. The peasant women still beat their flax at the river's edge to make linen thread, but, instead of weaving it, most took it to Ansbach to exchange for cloth. And some of the women were even trading their woolen thread there for cloth.

The decline of weaving here began when Count Poppo agreed to accept his share of Eschenbach's produce in thread instead of in cloth. This was practical, for it was easier to transport thread to Wertheim. But a village that does not weave its own cloth or make its own shoes has lost its independence. I feared that we might finally have to go to Ansbach for bread. Although it did not come to that in my lifetime, other forebodings of mine later became reality. Not only the villages, but also the towns were no longer self-sufficient. Through a shortsighted yielding to convenience, we not only placed our welfare in jeopardy but also gave up much of our freedom. Still Eschenbach, thank God, lagged behind most of Germany with regard to those changes and remained in many respects much as it was when I was a small boy. That is why, wherever I traveled, I was always glad to return.

I remember the summer primarily because of the renovation of the church, which was over two hundred years old and sadly in need of repair. On the outside all of the plaster was gone, exposing the bare stones to the frost, and most of plaster on the inside had fallen. Moreover one wall needed to be completely rebuilt. The workers included almost everyone in the village, even the children. When we were finished and the walls were white as snow inside and out, a talented monk from the Ansbach Monastery painted us a mural that shows Jesus blessing the animals, domestic and wild. It is famous throughout Franconia; people still travel here to see it.

The renovation was celebrated in great style. The children's choir sang three or four songs at mass—the music was beautiful—and afterward the entire village ate together, on tables that were set up on the meadow. Then a group of the older children put on a lively play about the Antichrist's defeat, that our priest had composed, using a Latin source. And finally there were several hours of dancing to Brother Andrew's fiddling and my singing. At nightfall I believe that all the villagers shared my feeling that the church should be repaired more often.

It was a gray day in early November when I, rather reluctantly, started out for Wartburg, and my spirits were not improved by a cold drizzle that began about an hour later. Shortly after passing through Ansbach, I overtook a group of some fifty riders, forty of whom were knights in armor. Since they were riding two or three abreast and the road was not wide, I could not pass. So I fell in line beside the last of the knights and began a conversation. I learned that the company consisted of the guards and the chief officials of Bishop Dietrich, the secular and spiritual head of the city-state of Würzburg, who was now returning from Rome.

"And what was his business there?" I asked.

"He attended a great congress, the Fourth Lateran Council," was the reply. "Hundreds of bishops, abbots, and representatives of kings, princes, and towns were there. They issued decrees against the abuses of the Church and those heresies that threaten the power of the clergy. At the urging of our bishop, they also proclaimed King Friedrich ruler of the Empire and again excommunicated Otto of Braunschweig."

"I'm glad to hear it," I said. "I know nothing of heresies and Church abuses but, having spent two winters at Count Hermann's Castle Wartburg, I've learned much about Empire affairs and I believe that Friedrich's new title will make it easier for him to keep the peace in Germany."

"That's just what our bishop maintained," declared the knight. "If you are returning to Wartburg, you will go by way of Würzburg. Why don't you join us? Dietrich sent a messenger ahead to get quarters for us. He'll be glad to have another warrior—bands of plundering Bohemian soldiers sometimes cross over into Franconia—and for three days you won't have to pitch your tent on a muddy field." Needless to say, I was delighted with the invitation, for even at the young age of forty-five, I was beginning to develop a strong aversion to cold and mud.

We spent the first night in a monastery, the second in a church, and the third in the bishop's castle in Würzburg; then I went on alone. When I reached Wartburg, I started to work on my Willehalm story at once, for I hoped to finish it before summer.

The most important event of the winter was the appearance of a bright, new star, a poet-composer who called himself Neidhart of Reuenthal. He did not come to Wartburg himself, but his songs did, and they were so popular that nothing else was sung at the dances, not even the compositions of Walther of Vogelweide. With the exception of a timid and impoverished knight—who had the same name as his creator—all of Neidhart's characters were peasants, not honest workers like those at Eschenbach, but crude and quarrelsome creatures whose speech was sometimes obscene. Most of the songs might be called grotesque parodies of courtly love songs.

These new lyrics were certainly clever and amusing and the melodies were delightful, but I was a little startled at their instant popularity. Abbot Hugo used to maintain that popular poetry was a faithful mirror of society, for if it did not at once reflect the nature of its audience, the latter would soon model itself after the poetry. And I wondered if these good lords and ladies would be corrupted by the characters they portrayed with such enthusiasm in the dances. However that may be, Neidhart was certainly talented and inventive.

Since he has doubtless been forgotten by now, it is fitting that I should sing for you the Neidhart song I like best, although it is really not typical:

Barren were the meadows and forsaken
until the summer came to warm and waken,
flowers pressed through grass and clover then.
Once again
summer now is opening the roses
and making lovely heath and glen.

Nightingale and thrush, we hear them singing,
with the sound the hills and vales are ringing.
They sing their songs of joyous summertime
as they climb.
May has brought us happiness and beauty:
the heath is blooming in its prime.

Spoke a maid, "The dew is on the heather,
see the splendor summer brings together.
The trees that in the wintertime were bare
everywhere
wave their leafy branches in the breezes.
The nightingales are singing there.

"Losa, hear the songs of birds resounding,
they greet the May from all the trees surrounding.
I fancy, we are free of winter now.
Wierat, thou
must dance more spritely, wouldst thou gain my favor,
beneath the linden's leafy bough.

"Spring's the time for each to choose a lover,
roses bloom beneath the forest's cover
and I shall have a crown of roses red
on my head
when I'm dancing hand in hand so gaily
with such a handsome knight," she said.

"Daughter, think no more of bold advances.
Shouldst thou encourage nobles at the dances,
who are not the sort for folk as we,
I foresee
thou willst have a lot of pain and trouble.
A sturdy peasant covets thee."

"Let a heifer wed the worthy farmer!
My hope is for a stately knight in armor.

Why should I take a peasant as my man?
Never can
I be happy with a rustic lover.
A knight alone will suit my plan."

"Daughter don't despise his lowly station
to win a stupid noble's admiration.
This has caused thy friends distress and pain.
All in vain
are thy promises, I tell thee truly,
thy wilfulness I never could restrain."

"Mother mine, stop scolding, and believe me,
I would love him though my friends should leave me,
I never hid my wishes, I recall.
One and all
may the people know whom I have chosen,
for he's the knight of Reuenthal."

Although, as I have said, I charged boldly and without delay into the struggle that would determine whether the western world would be Christian or Moslem, my progress was slow and difficult. There was a great deal of repetition in the real battles that I had fought, but audiences like variety, and I had employed all of the obvious tactics to achieve this in the account of the earlier conflict. To be sure, Rennewart and his terrible pole had great potential for novelty in this second battle, yet I could not have him defeat the countless enemies unassisted.

I struggled along and the Christians finally triumphed, but they were too grieved by their own losses for rejoicing. Willehalm was a generous victor—he freed the prisoners, let them take their slain leaders home for burial according to their own rites, and allowed them to keep their personal possessions—and I was an intrusive author, entering the story to reinforce Gyburg's plea for tolerance. "Is it not a sin," I asked, "when one considers men no better than cattle that one may slaughter, only because they have never heard the teaching of baptism? I declare that it surely is a sin, for, like us, they are human beings whom God has formed with his own hands."

Many found the ending too abrupt and complained that it leaves some loose threads. It has even been said that I died before the story was completed. While I deny this idle rumor as being quite unfounded, I do admit that the conclusion does have a significant fault: it does not say what happened to Rennewart. If he was killed in the battle, his body should be found so that he could be mourned and buried in a manner suitable to his station. If he was not slain, he should return to marry the daughter of the emperor. I intended the latter course and would have followed it, had fate not intervened.

When Count Hermann learned that I had come to the end of the French manuscript, he insisted on hearing the entire story. His friends and important vassals were invited to spend a week at Wartburg, and I was asked to read the work for two hours each evening. The response of the audience was most enthusiastic, and the count was so pleased by this that he was not very receptive when I criticized the ending and spoke of my plan to add to it.

"You can go home now," he said. "I'll have my scribe read it over again for me. If I agree to expand the ending, I'll send for you."

I left Wartburg two days later, feeling certain that a second reading would convince Hermann that Rennewart deserved a kinder destiny. At the count's request, I rode to Erfurt to join the retinue of a bishop of Thuringia, who was traveling to Rome and would take the same route as I as far as Ansbach. Since there was still some danger of attack from Bohemians, the good churchman would be glad to add another sturdy knight to his company. As for me, I was delighted. I had learned that bishops take a good cook along on their journeys and never camp out in bad weather.

During most of the trip I rode beside Sir Bertram of Ohrdrut, whom I had met at Hermann's court. A vassal of the count's, he had often been loaned to the bishop as a guard. "Why is the bishop going to Rome?" I asked him.

"It is not generally known," he replied, "but Pope Innocence is dying and will probably be dead before we reach Rome. Our bishop wants to be there early in order to work for the election of a successor who will not be as power-hungry as the present pope is. Innocence has tried, and usually with success, to dominate completely not only the German Church, but also the German states; most of our clergy oppose this."

I remembered at once Abbot Hugo's comments about the papacy and the Empire and his fear that, through the former, Germany would be dominated by Italians. "Perhaps the tide will turn," I thought.

Whenever the wind was chilly, the bishop wrapped himself in a large, white shawl on which words were embroidered with red silk thread. I became interested in knowing what they said and once managed to ride close enough to read them, but some were covered. Noticing my curiosity, the bishop spread the shawl out for me to see, and I read: "Inasmuch as you have done it unto the least of these my brothers, you have done it unto me."

"I believe I remember that Bible verse, your lordship," I said. "Do you have a particular reason for wearing it? I am not only a knight, but also a poet, and poets are by nature very inquisitive."

"I know who you are," was the reply, "and I'll gladly tell you the story:

Once when I was a young priest at Gotha, I became seriously ill. My belly became very swollen and I was constantly racked with pain. The doctors could do nothing. After several weeks of suffering, I was so exhausted that I fell asleep in spite of my agony and had a remarkable experience. I dreamed that I stood in front of the Christ Child and cried out: "How can I be free of this torment? What must I do to be cured?"

"Take me to Suhl!" the Child answered. "Take me to Suhl!"

I woke in wonderment. What did it mean? How could I take Him to Suhl? Then I remembered a small wooden madonna with Child that stood on a pedestal in a chapel of our church. It was made of two pieces of wood, and the infant could be lifted from the arms of the mother. "I'll take it to Suhl," I decided at once, "and see what happens."

The following morning I saddled my mule, tied a tent, a blanket, and some provisions behind the saddle, and rode to the church. I knew that the little statue would not be hard to get, for the chapel was usually empty. And indeed there was no one to see me when I slipped it into my sleeve and later into the saddle bag. Ordinarily the three-day journey through the mountains of the Thuringian Forest would have been too much for me, sick as I was, but, driven by pain and buoyed by hope, I managed to get there. What was I to do then? I went to the church and wandered about but found no fitting place to leave the statue in my sleeve. There should have been some sort of sign. "It was only a dream, an idle dream," I thought in bitter disappointment and departed for Gotha.

I was resting in the shade of a large oak, about a day's ride from Suhl, when an old man with a cane staggered from the road to the same tree and sat down, completely exhausted. "Where are you going?" I asked after he had gotten his breath.

"To Suhl," he replied. "I was living with my son in Oberhof, but he died. Now I am going to my other son, in Suhl. He is a good man and will take me in if I can get there."

It was clear to me that the poor old peasant couldn't walk twenty miles through the mountains. "He'll collapse and die within another five miles," I thought. "I'll try to do one more kind deed before I die myself."

We slept under the same blanket that night. Then I put the man in the saddle and led the mule back toward Suhl. It was not strong enough to carry us both. Night was falling when I entered the town, surprised that in my weakened condition I had been able to walk so far. The son was delighted to see his father. I accepted his offer of food and lodging and the next morning set out again for Gotha. The pain decreased as I rode and when I replaced the statue, three days later, it vanished and never returned. Then I remembered the verse you see on my shawl. I wear it there so that I may never forget those who are in need.

The bishop decided to stop for a day in Würzburg, to rest and to visit with an old friend, Bishop Dietrich. Luckily for the rest of us, the city was having its spring celebration, and we all were invited to take part. The festivities began with a sword fight between the May King, who was dressed in green and wore a crown of spring flowers, and the Winter Spirit, who wore a dark grey cloak and a hideous mask. When the latter was defeated and driven off, the May King led us all—the men and boys in their green-trimmed jackets, the women and girls in colorful summer attire, and us travelers in our Sunday best—out to the city common. Accompanied by a fiddle and a flute, we danced here all afternoon; there was plenty of wine for those who had to stop for rest. At our bishop's suggestion, I sang several of my compositions and led the company in the appropriate dances. I was applauded with enthusiasm.

The rest of my journey with the bishop was quite uneventful, and on the fourth day from Würzburg we reached Ansbach, where I parted from his company and went on alone to Eschenbach and my family. My chief task that summer was to oversee the improvement of the road between Eschenbach and Ansbach. Count Poppo and the prince of Ansbach had agreed to let their vassals in both places satisfy their annual obligations by supplying the labor needed to construct an all-weather, toll-free road for carts and wagons between the village and the town. Hitherto the road was passable only by horses and, in good weather, ox-carts. Although unhappy with this step toward facilitating commerce, I conscientiously carried out my orders. But then something happened that not only brought work on the road to a halt, but also stopped all traffic of any kind along it. This was the plague of 1215, that no Franconian will ever forget.

Early in July a peasant youth named Jurg hurried up the hill toward our house, stopped over two hundred feet from the door and called for me. When I appeared, he cried breathlessly: "There is plague in Ansbach! More than a score are sick."

"Have you been to the village?" I asked quickly.

"No," he replied. "I came straight here."

"Good," I said. "Was anyone with you in Ansbach?"

"No," was the answer, "I went alone."

"You must remain alone," I told him. "I'll have a tent put up at the top of the first ridge in the East Forest. There will be food and a bed in it. I'll arrange for food to be left regularly a hundred yards downhill from the tent. Do not come any closer than that to anyone." The youth left and I hurried down to the village and summoned all the peasants. We were indeed fortunate. I found that, during the preceding ten days, heavy rainfall had kept all of them at home; Jurg was the only one who had been in Ansbach in that time. Archers were posted at once to guard both entrances to the village and instructed to shoot anyone who ignored the order to go back.

We closed ourselves off completely from the outside world for four months and were spared. I was concerned about my friends not only in Ansbach, but also elsewhere: in Abenberg, Wertheim, Wildenberg, and Wartburg. However it was too dangerous to contact them; we had to wait. After the first heavy frosts of November, I sent one peasant toward Ansbach and another toward Abenberg to find out what they could about the plague while remaining at least two hundred feet from anyone. They reported that Abenberg had also heard of the plague in time and, by isolating itself, had had no illness. More than a hundred people had died in Ansbach, but there had been no cases since September. Both the prince's castle and the monastery had shut themselves in soon enough and had lost no one. Later I heard that most of the towns and villages to the north had suffered—but none had been utterly depopulated—and that many of the ill had recovered. Eventually I learned that all my friends and relatives had survived.

During the following year six or seven priests and monks traveled about Franconia preaching that the plague was God's punishment, calling upon us all to repent, and, like Jonah, threatening the entire land with utter destruction. But since my good Eschenbach peasants were too honest to believe that they had been saved by their righteousness, they held to the doctrine that the purposes behind the acts of God were beyond man's ability to fathom.

I received no message concerning the ending of the Willehalm story, but In the spring I was told that, soon after I left Wartburg, Count Hermann had taken ill—not with the plague—and had died the following winter. I may therefore answer those who criticize my work as being incomplete by maintaining that this too was an expression of the inscrutable will of God.

The Later Years

The first twelve years after I left Wartburg were spent in Eschenbach except for short periods of a week or so in which I gave readings of the Parzival or the Willehalm story at various courts in Franconia, Swabia, and Bavaria. I was quite in demand, for neither Baron Rupert nor Hermann's son Ludwig had allowed their manuscripts to be copied, so these romances could not be told outside of Wildenberg or Wartburg except by me. Now and then I also sang dance songs at festivals, but I did not compose any more of them. New lyrics would have been easy for me, but I have never been very inventive with respect to melodies. Had I lived closer to France or Italy, as did Hartmann of Aue and Walther of Vogelweide, I could have borrowed foreign tunes, but here in Franconia these sources were denied me.

For a while I considered composing another courtly romance, one dealing with the love of Sigune and Schionatulander and their sad fate. Those familiar with the Parzival narrative will remember that the hero encountered Sigune several times while she was mourning the death of her lover. Whereas the adventures of Gawain in the story give a comic view of the "service of a lady" (the winning of a lady's love by performing deeds of valor for her sake), the appearances of Sigune emphasize a tragic aspect of this romantic convention.

Since there seemed to be considerable interest in these star-crossed lovers, I composed an introductory chapter about them: their childhood, their early love, the nature of "courtly love," Sigune's request that Schionatulander win her by valiant deeds, and the youth's departure to serve in the armed forces of an oriental monarch. Then I prepared a short sketch that presented the seemingly harmless episode that led to Schionatulander's death: After the latter's return, he was in the forest with his sweetheart when a hound ran past, dragging a very long ribbon-like leash. The youth caught the hound and they found writing on the leash that told a most interesting love story, but before Sigune got to the end of it, the hound escaped. She then asked Schionatulander to win her by bringing her the leash, a "service" that eventually led to his death and her bitter remorse.

I added these two selections to the program at many of the Parzival readings in hope of finding a sponsor who would commission the romance, but none appeared. Although I was disappointed at the time, I later decided that the story was not suitable for me. I confess to having been something of a joker; I was at my best in the Parzival story when I was making fun of the characters or myself. Such humor would certainly be out of place in a thoroughly tragic tale like that I had planned.

One might think that, after spending three winters at Hermann's court, I would find Eschenbach frightfully dull, but this was not the case. Besides family matters, there were village affairs to be dealt with, and there was hunting. Although I was never as devoted to the sport as my father was, with the years I lost my boyhood sensitivity about killing and found the chase a pleasant diversion. Actually it was more than that; it was our sole source of red meat. We were as dependent on the deer and hares of the North Forest for meat as the peasants were on the beasts in their pastures. I had never left Eschenbach in the fall without leaving behind enough smoked venison to last until summer.

Hunting was not always enjoyable. Indeed none of my experiences in three campaigns was as frightening as an encounter I had with a certain wild boar. One day a peasant ran up to the house to report that this beast had broken into his pen and killed his domestic boar. I quickly seized my hunting spear, stuck a long knife in my belt, and hurried out to saddle my horse. I was just starting off with the hounds when my wife ran from the house with mail stockings. "Take these," she said, and placed them on the saddle behind me.

The hounds reached the peasant's farmyard ahead of me and pursued the boar as he ran toward the forest. I could not see them because of a hedgerow, but galloped in the direction of the baying and was only some eighty feet behind when they came into view. I was amazed! I had never seen such a boar. He must have weighed over six hundred pounds! The hounds were aware that this was no ordinary prey and were unusually cautious. Had it been a stag, they would have been leaping at its legs and shoulders to bring it down, but, although they feigned such attacks in order to slow the monster, they always dodged away from his long, razor-sharp tusks.

Before I could overtake the boar, he entered the forest and disappeared into a dense thicket of vines and briars. The hounds surrounded this patch of undergrowth but made no serious attempt to enter. They obviously considered that the next step was up to me. I dismounted and circled the boar's stronghold several times, looking for a weak point but found none. I believe that I would have called off the hounds then and left for home, had it not been for the arrival of a dozen peasant youths who had raced after us. What was I to do? My father had become a legend in the village, and they clearly expected like valor of me. It is not easy to be the son of one who knew no fear.

I had conducted myself well in battle. But then I was wearing armor and usually facing a single foe; if outnumbered, I could trust my good steed to get me out of danger. Here I would push through brambles toward an unseen enemy that was as well armed as I and much larger, and there could be no tactical retreat. Frightened as never before, I put on the mail stockings that my foresighted wife had given me, held my spear ready, and forced my way into the thicket. I was surprised and a little encouraged to see that the hounds to my left and right were also making their way through the brambles.

The boar's attack was sudden and fierce. I had just time to plunge my spear into his shoulder before being hurled to the ground. The mail saved my legs when I was struck, but, prostrate, I would have been disemboweled at once had the hounds beside me not seized the monster by the ears and the others, that had crept up behind it, not sunk their teeth into his flanks and hind legs. With eight hounds holding on desperately, the monster raged about, thrashing here and there in a demonic fury that threatened to destroy us all, until I managed to leap astride him and cut his throat with my knife. What rash and senseless things men and hounds will do to save their pride! But, though bloody and tattered, we all survived. I asked the peasants to get a pair of oxen and drag the boar up to my house, then led my victorious warriors home with heads and tails held high.

At the same time my sense of relief and satisfaction was mixed with regret, for a magnificent creature, the king of Franconia's beasts was dead, and the forest might never again see his like. Yet in a sense the great boar never died, for he became an important and apparently permanent figure of the local mythology. A mere thirty years later, he had more than doubled in size and could be conquered only by all of the hounds and men of Eschenbach. His spirit roamed the forest at night and was sometimes seen as a dark, threatening shadow in the moonlight.

The boar was not the only large beast to invade Eschenbach; once a bear came. I'll tell you about it. The church was on the edge of the village, close to the forest, and the priest, who dearly loved honey, had four beehives that he kept at the far end of the churchyard. This meant that grave digging and burials had to be carried on in the twilight or by lantern-light after the bees had retired, for they did not care for such activities close to their homes. But the peasants adjusted so fully to this situation that, many years after the beehives were gone, they still buried their dead in the late evening or at night.

One day a boy ran up to my door crying: "A bear is eating the priest's honey!" I had just returned from a ride, and my steed was still saddled, so it took me less than a minute to get my spear and turn loose the hounds. Dashing into the churchyard, we saw the bear sitting beside a broken beehive and so busy eating with one paw and waving the bees away from his nose and eyes with the other that he had not heard us approach. But, at the sight of us, he sprang up, scrambled over the wall that enclosed the churchyard, and ran toward the forest. The hounds and I followed close behind. Although it may have looked as if we were pursuing the bear, in reality we were chiefly interested in escaping from the thousands of angry bees. I don't remember whether or not I had intended to kill the honey-thief but, if so, I gave up the idea at once. For in order to do this, we would have needed to bring the beast to a halt, and neither I nor the hounds considered this feasible.

We chased him far into the woods, then went home to nurse our stings. Not having a thick coat of hair like the hounds, I got by far the worst of it. Still, he who is responsible for the welfare of others must expect some pain. The affair turned out fairly well for all concerned: the priest lost only one of his beehives, the bear got plenty of honey and escaped with his life, and the hounds and I had the satisfaction of knowing that, although vastly outnumbered, we had done our duty.

The only other wild beasts to trouble Eschenbach in my time were foxes and a wolf. I believe that, on the whole, the foxes were useful to the peasants, for they were an ever-present reminder that one needs to be industrious and vigilant to be successful. With regard to raising chickens, this means that one must lock them in a secure henhouse at night and protect them with a sturdy and well-tended brush fence during the day. These brush fences—about which scholars know nothing—were made by setting posts firmly in the ground and interweaving them with branches. They were supposed to be inspected daily.

The lone wolf did nothing to harm the villagers or their stock—indeed, no one ever saw him—but for a while he caused many of the former much concern. He would go to the bald top of a neighboring hill, when the moon was full and the sky was clear, and howl with a fine baritone voice. This excited all the dogs in Eschenbach, including mine, who would respond with barks or howls that varied from high tenor to low bass. This delightful and profound litany of priest and choir often would continue for two or three hours.

The peasants did not share my pleasure and suggested that I do something about it. "He upsets the hounds, and they make such a racket that nobody can sleep," one of them complained. "Moreover there is something eerie about this howling from a wolf that's never been seen and about his effect on our dogs. It's not natural and it might be dangerous. My mother told me that a wolf, or something that sounded like a wolf, howled the night before my grandfather died."

I tried to reassure them and defend the wolf. "It's just a wild beast," I replied, "and it's his nature to howl at the moon. He shouldn't be held responsible for the howling of others. If he attacked your cattle, I would hunt him down, but since he has not done so, we should live and let live. Suppose he is not an ordinary wolf—which I'm sure he is—but something that can't be seen, what could I do? I have no power over such beings."

For several months tension and outright fear grew in the village, but there were no dire consequences of the howling, and the peasants gradually began to accept and even welcome it. "There will be a full moon tonight and the sky is clear," they would say. "The wolf will howl." This continued for about seven years. Then a full moon shone down from a cloudless sky and no sound came from the hill, only an oppressive silence. No one slept that night or the following ones. "It's not natural," a peasant told me. "It's an ill omen. Some grave misfortune is going to befall us." We never heard the wolf again, and we all—humans and hounds—missed him. None more than I.

I believe that it was the following spring when the black swan appeared. The long pool in the stream that flowed past the village was a stopover for swans as they migrated north and south; a dozen or so stayed with us for about two weeks in April and November. Their arrival was an important event in the life of Eschenbach, and most of the peasants went down to the pool to greet them. One of the birds this spring was a large male, coal-black, and as elegant and regal a creature as ever lived. "What a swan!" I exclaimed to my wife. "Did you ever see the like?"

"No," she replied, "but it's not really a swan. As a poet you should know that. It is surely a Moorish prince who has assumed this form while he goes north to find a bride." In truth, his every movement revealed the self-assurance of one born to rule, and the other swans treated him as a monarch. They moved from his path as he swam along and even seemed to bow as they did so. After the usual stay, the black swan flew north, followed by the others, who remained a respectable distance behind. But he was not forgotten, and there was considerable discussion among the villagers as to whether he was likely to return. In November he did come back—accompanied by a white mate with a bright-red bill to whom he appeared quite devoted and two black-and-white offspring. The family remained for two weeks, then flew south with the others.

For five years the black swan and his mate stopped at Eschenbach on their migrations, and the peasants of Eschenbach were proud of their unusual guest. Sometimes people came from neighboring villages and Ansbach to see him. In November of the sixth year the black swan and his mate arrived, contrary to their custom, several days later than the others, and there were no offspring with them. We soon noticed that something was wrong with the black swan: he moved with his usual dignity and grace while in the water, but could hardly get about at all on land and only left the pool for the night. During the day he stayed in the water and fed on the plants that he could reach from there. His mate often brought him seeds or grass from the adjoining meadow.

One evening when he crawled from the pool I was close enough to see what was wrong: the shaft of an arrow protruded from his back. The Moorish prince had been shot.

What was to be done? Since he always rested at the water's edge, it would not be easy to catch him and remove the arrow. And, if I should catch him, would the ensuing struggle and operation not do more harm than good? Regretfully I decided to do nothing. After a longer stay than was their custom, the great black swan and his snow-white mate flew south. He never returned, but I think we saw her for many more years. All of the swans migrated in pairs but one female with a bright-red bill. She traveled alone.

It was in the late fall, after the death of the black swan, that the great snowstorm struck Eschenbach. The sky became overcast in midmorning, and the snow began to fall. It came down so thick that one could see nothing, not even a hand against one's nose, only a gray blanket that pressed in from all sides, stifling sound and making breathing difficult. There was no wind. The man in the open was completely isolated, divorced from all else, even from himself, for thought seemed walled in and benumbed. It was frightening. Fortunately none of the villagers was in the fields at the time; otherwise he might not have found his way home. Even those in their own yards had trouble groping along to a door. At first we felt secure inside, because it seemed impossible that such a snow fall could last longer than a few minutes. But the minutes stretched into hours, and we became aware of a new danger.

When the beams of my house began to creak overhead, my son went out to lessen the weight on the roof. Standing on a ladder that he could not see, he used an invisible and soundless hay rake to clear invisible tiles, while I struggled down to the village to warn the peasants. I quickly lost all sense of direction, and it was pure chance that caused me to stumble against the side of a house. I went completely around it in search of a door, delivered my warning, and continued on to the next dwelling. Luckily all had ladders and rakes. I returned as I went, but was afraid to leave the last house for fear of losing my way. However my son had foreseen this danger and was sounding a hunting horn, one that ordinarily could be heard for a mile but now was barely audible at a hundred yards.

At about five o'clock the storm ceased as abruptly as it had begun, but our troubles were not over. The snow was nearly five foot deep, and the cattle were out on the river pasture, the far end of which was a mile away. There was no time to lose, for the animals, over their heads in snow, would be hard to find, and many might die of exposure or suffocation before morning. My charger was strong and tall and, by rearing and leaping, was able to bring me to the village, where all able-bodied men and the four oxen that were not in the pasture were immediately mobilized. My steed led the file until it was exhausted. From then on the strongest men, leading oxen, took turns at the front. In an hour and a half we had fought our way to and through the pasture and had begun the search for the cattle.

Because of the absence of drifts, they were not too hard to find. They had crowded together in three groups according to their kind—cows, goats, and sheep—and elevations in the snow betrayed their presence. A full moon, now shining down on the snow, gave us almost the light of day. With fourteen oxen in the lead, the return trip was easy, even for the smallest sheep, but there was still much to do, for a path had to be forced to each barn. Since four buildings had collapsed, some peasants and animals were quartered with neighbors. It was midnight before we were through and I, leading my weary steed, had struggled up to our house.

The following day was clear and bright. The men were busily raising the four buildings while the children were merrily running unseen along the paths we had made. Although the village—people, dwellings, and cattle—had teetered on the brink of disaster, the peril was forgotten in a week, and the event had become a cherished legend and milestone of time. From then on, everything was dated according to the great snow fall of 1226.

After the death of Abbot Hugo I continued to visit the Ansbach monastery, to see my friends there and to keep up on the news of Germany and the Empire. Once I was present at a performance of a minstrel who had formerly been a priest. His program consisted mainly of Latin songs, that I, of course, did not understand. They evoked such laughter from his audience that I was not greatly surprised on being told later that they were wittily amorous, sometimes even obscene. But the minstrel also sang several German songs by a composer of whom I had never heard. "He is a Styrian nobleman, named Ulrich of Liechtenstein," the minstrel informed us, "a wealthy lord who is very influential in the affairs of his country." I liked his compositions. They had the same lighthearted charm as those of Heinrich of Veldeke although both the lyrics and the melodies were more sophisticated. This is a May-Day song I still remember:

Little birds in forest bowers
sing as one their sweetest lay.
On the meadow pretty flowers
bloom against the light of May.
So now blooms my self-esteem
in the thought of her devotion
which enriches my emotion
as a beggar by a dream.

High the hopes I hold and nourish
in the presence of her charms
that my fortune still may flourish
till I hold her in my arms.
Such desire is all my joy.
Now may God in fullest measure
grant that these, the hopes I treasure,
she I love will not destroy.

May the gentle one I cherish
free of fault or broken vow
never cause this dream to perish
which is all I have for now.
May my pleasure never wane,
may I not in tears awaken,
may I laugh, with courage taken
from the solace I shall gain.

Pleasant thoughts and fond desires,
these are all the joys I sing.
But my love for her requires
little more if I may bring
both into her company
that she willingly may tender
something of her charm and splendor
and be ever kind to me.

Blessed May, your gentle weather
warms the whole world with its kiss.
You and all the world together
bring me not a mite of bliss.
For what pleasure could you give
were the lovely one not near me?
She alone has power to cheer me,
from her solace I must live.

After the performance I learned from Brother Andrew that Pope Honorius was quite favorably disposed toward the monastic orders and had confirmed the legitimacy of two new brotherhoods, the Dominicans and the Franciscans. Moreover, he was less ambitious with regard to secular power than his predecessor, Innocence, had been and therefore got along rather well with Friedrich. But their relations were becoming somewhat strained because the emperor, beset with revolts in Sicily and Lombardy, was quite hesitant about embarking on a campaign to drive the Saracens from the Holy Land. This Crusade was the chief goal of the pope, and he was constantly urging all the kings and princes of Christendom to support it. Brother Andrew was of the opinion that Friedrich should settle down in Swabia, let Lombardy and Sicily go their way, and leave the Crusade to the English and French. "What has Germany to do with these foreign lands!" he exclaimed. Remembering that my father had died in an unsuccessful Crusade, I shared his view.

The Crusade was much in my thoughts in the following months and, when the news came that Friedrich had married the daughter of the Christian king of the land of Jerusalem, I was certain that the emperor would soon lead an army to free its capital and holy city from the Saracens. So I was not surprised when Count Poppo's messenger arrived in the spring of 1228 to say that I should send my son, Wolfram the Younger, to Kelheim in Bavaria to serve in the army that Duke Ludwig was to lead to Palestine. "Give my respects to the count," I told him, "and say that I shall go myself and leave my son to care for Eschenbach. It will be in good hands for he has in fact been in charge of matters here for several years. And Duke Ludwig will lose nothing by taking an old veteran of two campaigns in place of a younger but less experienced knight."

I did not reach this decision because my father had gone with Barbarossa in my place but for other reasons. One was that at fifty-eight I felt a real need to have a last adventure, a great adventure, before I died; the other reason was that I had gotten interested in my descendants. I wanted to be remembered as the first of a line of Wolframs of Eschenbach that would continue for a hundred years or more, and my son was in a better position than I to further this dream.

Two weeks later I set out for Kelheim, on my charger and leading a packhorse. In four days I reached the Danube, the largest and most beautiful river I had ever seen, and soon afterward joined the other vassals of Count Poppo in a large encampment below the duke's castle. I learned here that we were not to follow Barbarossa's route down to Greece, but would ride through the Alps to Venice, where we would set sail for Acre. The emperor would sail from Brindisi with an army of Lombards, Swabians, and Rhinelanders and meet us there.

Our army, consisting of some two thousand knights and a like number of foot soldiers, followed the Danube to the Isar, then moved up the Isar valley into Tyrol. What magnificent mountains the Alps are! Compared to them, our Franconian and Thuringian mountains are mole hills! Up and up we crept and, when we reached the highest point of a pass, the snow-clad peaks still towered high above us. Stretching for miles ahead and behind me, our column wound around the mountains like a great serpent.

This was the wondrous land of fable. As I rode along, my eyes searched the Alpine meadows for the rose garden where the mighty dwarf-king Laurin fought the Gothic King Dietrich of Verona, also known as Theodoric the Great. I looked at the foot of each high cliff for the tall linden under which the Lombard King Ortnit encountered Alberich, another dwarf-king, who was invisible to all except the wearer of a certain ring. I wondered which of the forest trails we passed was the one by which the fierce giant pair, Helle and Runze, waited for unfortunate travelers, and every mountain lake seemed the one guarded by the fire-breathing serpent of legend. Several of the caves we passed fit the description of the one in which the heroic Wolfdietrich slew the dragons, and two or three of the lofty peaks reminded me of the hollow mountain in which Lady Liebgard was imprisoned. I was almost certain that one of the castles I saw was that of the beautiful enchantress who could give the valley below the appearance of a large lake and make the opposite mountain seem to be covered with raging flames.

To rest horses and men, we camped three days in Innsbruck and two days in Brunico, but after we reached the valley of the Piave, traveling was easier and we pressed on every day until we came to the sea. How well I remember my first sight of the sea: nothing but water as far as the eye could reach! The earth was indeed vast. We camped at the mouth of the river while the duke and his retainers rode down the coast to Venice to make arrangements for our passage.

We sailed as an armada of at least forty ships and, although the waters were said to be infested with Saracen galleys, we arrived without incident at Acre. The city and the adjoining plain were full of Christian troops—English, French, Knights Templar, Teutonic Knights, and perhaps others—all waiting for the emperor. Some had the true crusading zeal to wrest the Holy City from the Saracens, a few (like my father) enjoyed battle for its own sake, some (like myself) wanted to see strange lands, most would have stayed at home if they had had a choice. When I encountered an Englishman who could speak German, I asked why he and his countrymen were there. "Because of a vision," he replied. "I did not see it myself but many others did. The Lord showed Himself in the sky as when crucified: nailed to a shining cross and pierced with a spear. Who could doubt why He did so?"

A Parisian told of a different sign in the heavens: A famous astronomer of Toledo had predicted that on the first of August all the planets would be in concourse over Palestine, which meant that the land would then be devastated by a great earthquake. "We'll still be here then," the Frenchman said nervously. "The pope should have waited with this Crusade till fall."

For the most part the different armies kept to themselves and displayed little harmony. Indeed a disagreement of the Templars and the Teutonic Knights grew into a pitched battle, that ended only when Duke Ludwig led us Germans between the combatants and threatened to attack them both. The commander of the Frenchmen was quite critical of his action. "Why couldn't that meddling Bavarian have let those arrogant monks kill each other off!" he was heard to exclaim.

We waited for the emperor for several months, and our provisions were almost exhausted by the time he arrived. His departure from Italy had been delayed because a plague had broken out in his army. Among those who died was the kind and gentle Ludwig of Thuringia, with whom I had become acquainted at Wartburg while composing my Willehalm story. Friedrich himself had been seriously ill but had quickly recovered.

The emperor brought a large army and ample supplies and was welcomed with enthusiasm by all of the troops. The foreigners were especially pleased to find that their commander spoke French and English as well as German and Latin; he also knew Arabic. We were hurriedly making preparations for the campaign when a ship bearing a delegate from the newly elected Pope Gregory entered the harbor. He carried letters from the pope that proclaimed the excommunication of the emperor for not having sailed sooner and forbade all Christians to assist him in any way. Fortunately the only ones who took the order to heart were the Churchmen, most of whom had not planned to take part in the fighting in any event. Even the Teutonic Knights, but not the Templars, followed his banner.

We went first to Jaffa to fortify it well, then began our advance on Jerusalem, but before we reached the city, the sultan sent messengers inviting Friedrich to a conference. This lasted for about a week and ended by the Saracens giving up the Holy City as well as Bethlehem, Nazareth, and much of the rest of the territory they held in Palestine. I suppose that the bloodless victory was a surprise to everyone but Friedrich. It was rumored that the sultan had such bitter enemies among his own relatives that he did not feel prepared to oppose us. In any case, it was not difficult for me to overcome my regret at having to leave the land without any battle tales to take home.

There were no celebrations in the churches, for the priests were not happy at Friedrich's success. This was due primarily to his being excommunicated, but also because he had promised that the Saracens in the cities controlled by the Christians would be allowed to keep their mosques and worship as they pleased. The granting of such liberty, they maintained, was heretical, and, when the emperor entered the temple of Solomon (that the Saracens called the mosque of Omar) to be confirmed as king of the state of Jerusalem, the head of the Christian church in Palestine, the patriarch, would not place the crown on his head. But this troubled him little; he took the crown from the altar himself and placed it on his head, as Charlemagne had done at the founding of the Empire. The head of the Teutonic Knights followed this act with words of praise for the new king. After the ceremony Friedrich remained for several weeks in Jerusalem to set up his government there, but he sent most of his army back to Acre so that it would be closer to its source of supplies, the ships that came regularly from Italy.

The Templars appeared to accept the situation in good grace, for they invited the emperor to their castle on the edge of the city to celebrate the liberation of Jerusalem and his coronation. They had just moved back into this stronghold from which they had been driven over forty years previously. On the recommendation of Duke Ludwig, who had heard my romances, I was among the three hundred knights chosen to be Friedrich's guard of honor on this occasion. Just as we were leaving his headquarters, three Saracens rode up and asked to see the emperor. "We have a letter for him," they said. There was a short delay, then we rode to the castle.

I was fortunate enough to be among the hundred members of the guard to accompany Friedrich into the great hall for dinner; the rest were to be fed in the courtyard. We had just sat down to eat when the emperor asked for silence. "You will all be interested in a letter that I have just received," he said and read the following: "Most honored Sultan al-Kamil, On the evening of the twenty-first of February your chief enemy, Emperor Friedrich, will be at the castle of the Templars with a relatively small guard. Moreover, the greatest part of his army has returned to Acre. The castle gates will be open and, if you should choose to seize him, neither I nor the men of my order will interfere. Your friend, Armand of Perigord, Grand Master of the Knights Templar."

There was not a sound in the hall while one could have counted ten, so great was our shocked surprise. Then the two hundred and fifty men in the hall leaped to their feet, sword in hand. The Templar across the table from me was a little slow, which cost him his life, for I cut his head open as he rose. I had never seen such a melee. Those of the emperor's guard who were closest to him at once formed a protective circle around him, the rest of us fought for our lives with foes on all sides. For the moment we were outnumbered, but when our comrades rushed in from the courtyard, our force was so superior that the Templars soon dropped their swords and surrendered. Friedrich had Armand and three of his lieutenants hanged from the tower but spared the others, for he did not know to what extent they were parties to the treason.

"I regret the losses you suffered," the emperor told us later. "I did not tell you about the letter because I feared that among you there might be a traitor who would warn the Templars and give Armand a chance to flee."

"Perhaps," I thought, "but the emperor has a flair for the dramatic and, even at the cost of some lives, could not miss a chance to surprise us all."

Soon afterwards Friedrich appointed a viceroy, ordered that Jerusalem's walls be repaired, and sailed back to Sicily. Duke Ludwig's army returned to Acre and embarked not long afterward. I was not sorry to leave, for Palestine had been something of a disappointment: neither the countryside nor the cities could be compared to those in Franconia. Still, I had trod the same soil as Alexander the Great, Julius Caesar, Barbarossa, the twelve apostles, and Christ Himself; I was now not only a poet but a world-traveler.

Before our departure I went to the mass grave where Sir Eberhard and the rest of Duke Friedrich's knights were buried. "Father," I said solemnly, "I have been a small part of the army that fulfilled the mission for which you gave your life."

"Don't talk nonsense, son," I seemed to hear him reply. "I came for the same reason you came: adventure. And if you keep looking for it, you will share my fate. But I, at least, have no regrets."

We sailed for Triest, rather than Venice, and arrived there in about two weeks. The view of the city from the sea is truly impressive. It sits on a narrow shelf at the foot of a mountain so steep that it looks like a gigantic cliff. Since it was Sunday, masses were held from dawn till dark so that we all could attend. The cathedral there is very old and much different from any other I had seen; they say that it had once been a Roman temple in which heathen gods were worshipped. During the services an artist was working at one side on a large mosaic, which interested me more than the mass.

Starting out early the following morning, we rode along the shore and did not ascend the mountains until a day after we passed the north end of the sea and crossed the river that flows into it there. These Carinthian Alps are perhaps not quite as high as those in Tyrol, but they are just as steep, wild, and rugged, and they have similar legends of dwarfs, giants, and dragons. In addition, there is said to be a fairy queen here, one who lives in a hidden valley and rules over mountain dwarfs. And any wanderer who chances to enter that valley must remain there; no one can leave.

Once more we made our way toward Innsbruck, but from the east, rather than from the south, and again we rested our steeds there for three days before moving on. Since Duke Ludwig was a guest of Count Wilhelm, the ruler of Tyrol, during this time, some of the duke's men were invited to attend the entertainment each evening at the count's castle. A Carinthian poet, named Heinrich of Türlin, was reciting his Arthurian romance, that he called "The Crown." And Ludwig saw to it that I—also a romancer—was present. It was a highly imaginative work, the hero of which was the same Gawain who played an important role in my Parzival narrative. Indeed, the latter part of the romance dealt with a search for the Grail that was based on my story. The chief difference was in the nature of the Grail company. In my version it was a divinely established society whose purpose it was to provide rulers for lands in need of them; in Heinrich's work it was a community of living dead who suffered under a curse.

The surroundings of Innsbruck are truly impressive. If I were to live any place other than Eschenbach, I would want it to be in the high mountains; perhaps in the valley of the fairy queen. But then I was eager to get home, and was glad to start out again. For a while, at his request, I rode beside Duke Ludwig while we discussed Heinrich's work and its relation to mine. Since he was well acquainted with both German and French romances, I greatly enjoyed the conversation.

After we entered Bavaria, the different companies began to leave the army and go their separate ways. I left with Count Poppo's other vassals and traveled with them for two days, then went on alone. When I rode up to the modest house above my native village, I had been absent on the Crusade exactly a year and a half and had fought only Christians.

Two years of Eschenbach's pleasant rural routine had passed when a messenger arrived from Duke Ludwig asking me to come in September and recite my romances in the evenings at a great festival that he was holding; I would also sing at the dances on those afternoons that were not devoted to jousting. Three weeks later I set out for Kelheim and thereby became a witness to the most notorious unsolved murder to be committed in Germany during my lifetime.

Before going further, I must tell more about the duke, one of the most powerful of the German princes. He was several years younger than I and had ruled his land since his eighteenth birthday. As a vigorous supporter of the Hohenstaufens, he had helped carry out the imperial ban imposed on his cousin, Otto of

Wittelsbach, the murderer of King Philip, and had destroyed his castle. As a reward, he was given all of his cousin's hereditary estates.

Later, during the short, contested reign of Emperor Otto, Ludwig received from the latter the Möhringen estate and the recognition of the right of his descendants to inherit Bavaria. In return he supported Otto for a time in his contest with Friedrich for the crown of Germany, but later he shifted his loyalty to the Hohenstaufen and was rewarded with the Palatinate. And when Friedrich got his minor son, Heinrich, elected king of Germany, Duke Ludwig was appointed regent.

But the Pope's excommunication of Friedrich created serious problems for Duke Ludwig as soon as he returned from the Crusade, for the bishops in Bavaria were powerful allies of Gregory. Ludwig therefore denounced the emperor and rejected his authority. This proclamation brought on an immediate attack by the rash King Heinrich, now of age, who realized that his own position was threatened. Duke Ludwig was able to repel the assault, and Heinrich, waiting perhaps for help from his father, did not launch another.

This was the situation when I arrived at Kelheim. I wondered why, considering the possibility of further battles, Ludwig was having a festival. Perhaps he wanted the young king to see how many powerful friends he had. I related the romances, sang for dances in the afternoons, and, when not performing, watched the great lords. I was particularly interested in four of them: Ludwig's sullen, twenty-four-year-old son Albrecht and three austere Bavarian bishops. I had seen the types before: ambitious sons who were eager to be the lord of a court instead of an appendage to one and highborn Churchmen who resented the dominant position of secular princes. "A less forceful and wily duke would have trouble with these bishops," I told myself.

One afternoon I was standing on a parapet of the castle and looking down at the river below when I saw Duke Ludwig walking across the bridge. Then I noticed someone start toward him from the other side. When the duke came near, the man bowed and stood aside as if to let him pass. But as soon as they were close to each other, the stranger drew a dagger, stabbed Ludwig twice, and ran back across the bridge. Here he sprang on a horse that had been tethered to a bush and galloped away. It must have been four or five minutes before there was any pursuit; by then he had vanished. No one had recognized the man or even noticed him before the murder. He had chosen a good time for such a deed, for there were many unfamiliar faces among the thousand visitors camped along the river bank.

One thing was clear: the stranger was a paid assassin. But who had hired him? There were many suspects. The bishops at once loudly accused the excommunicated emperor; some were sure it was the young King Heinrich, who had failed to subdue the duke in battle; others believed that it might well be Otto of Wittelbach's son, whose ancestral estates had gone to Ludwig; I thought of Ludwig's impatient son and the power-hungry bishops. Who was responsible for this cowardly murder? I loved mysteries and spent many hours on this one.

The emperor was easily eliminated. Friedrich was not a man of passion; everything he did was a well-reasoned, astute step toward a specific goal. He knew that Ludwig was no threat to him and that, in siding with the pope, he was merely bending to the pressure of his bishops. His son Heinrich, on the other hand, was hotheaded and did not have the best of advisers, but still he would know that he would be immediately suspected of the death of a duke with whom he had recently fought. And he would also be aware that his father's influence would not save his crown if the German princes became convinced of his guilt.

As for Otto's unfortunate son, why would he wait twenty-three years to avenge the loss of the family estates? During this long period, there would have been many opportunities to slay his kinsman. No, he was not the conspirator. This left the restless Albrecht and the bishops. Patricide was by no means unheard of among German nobility, but Ludwig's son did not seem to be a fool. His father was fifty-seven years old and not likely to live another ten years, and at that time Albrecht would be only thirty-four years of age, rather young for a duke. Moreover, Ludwig, as a sensible ruler, would soon be gradually shifting power to his son and training him to govern well.

Only the Churchman remained, but I was not sure that I had solved the murder until six months later. Then I heard that the bishops with lies, threats, and flattery had gotten the inexperienced young duke to grant them immunity from all the secular controls that had prevailed in Bavaria since Charlemagne; they were now his peers. This could never have happened if Ludwig had lived or if his son had been older. The bishops were those with the most to gain and the ones who could not wait. Although very pleased at having identified the instigators of this villainy, I did not boast about it. Indeed, I said nothing to anyone. I would be too easy a target for an assassin.

Four years after the death of Ludwig, Heinrich's rashness got him into trouble again. He had long been annoyed at the widely held assumption that he was little more than his father's viceroy, and he finally decided to show the world that he was not a king in name only. After consulting with advisers who were as reckless as he, he proclaimed the independence of Germany from both Empire and emperor. In response, Friedrich sent messengers to all the German princes, asking them to show their loyalty. The result was an overwhelming display of unity. Warriors gathered in all the German lands and streamed southward to support the emperor. I joined the Franconian troops when they reached Ansbach. Moving on, we merged first with the Thuringian host, then with a great army of Saxons. Before the flood of knights entered Swabia, it grew with the addition of the Bavarians and Easterners, then was united with the troops of Hessians and Rhinelanders that had ridden down in the west. But the mighty host of Germans, the greatest to assemble in my lifetime, came too late to affect the outcome, for Heinrich's own Swabian lords had already defeated the king's men and forced him to retreat to Castle Hohenstaufen.

When Friedrich crossed the Alps with a small company of retainers, the castle was already under siege. As soon as his father arrived to protect him, Heinrich surrendered and was banished by a forgiving, but not indulgent, emperor to a small estate in southern Italy. More than sixty thousand troops looked on as their former king rode out of his ancestral castle and was conducted toward the Alps. Once more the integrity of Germany and the Empire had been preserved, and I was optimistic about their future.

My story ends with the return to Eschenbach. I don't know what happened there. It might have been a fall from my steed, or perhaps the journey was too strenuous for an old man. As for my present existence, I have none. Maybe Wolfram of Eschenbach's soul is somewhere being rewarded or punished for his deeds on earth. I do not know. But what you see before you is only a memory, a rather inquisitive memory that rises now and then from the grave and, sitting on this stone, counts the centuries by noting the growth and fall of the trees nearby and keeps somewhat abreast of the times by listening to the conversations of the lovers who meet here on summer nights.

As you may know, nothing came of my dream of founding a modest Eschenbach dynasty. The names of my wife and son appear on the stones next to mine, but there are no other Wolframs here. Still, I consider myself fortunate. I lived in the best of times and was close to some of the best of people. Sir Eberhard was as brave as any hero of legend; mother had no peer as a storyteller; my wife was as loving and loyal as Hartmann's heroine Enite; Abbot Hugo had the wisdom of Solomon. Moreover, I was a friend of Walther of Vogelweide, the greatest lyric poet of Germany; I campaigned with King Philip and Emperor Friedrich, the two most learned and astute of monarchs; and, after seven centuries, my romances are read by such scholars as yourself.

About the Author

J.W. Thomas is an emeritus professor of medieval German literature at the University of Kentucky. He is the author of twenty-five books and numerous articles dealing with his field of specialization. This is his first novel.